"The land, the water, and the animals are not here to play with. It was given to us to look after and protect. The land is the only thing that we depend on for everything, and it is not for sale."

AMEN TAILBONE

N D E H

A Dene Celebration

With photographs by René Fumoleau

ISBN 0-9691841-0-7

Published by:
The Dene Nation
P.O. Box 2338
Yellowknife
Denendeh
N.W.T.
XOE 1HO

We thank the Canada Council, the Department of
Education of the Government of the Northwest
Territories, and the Oblate Fathers for their financial
assistance in the production of this celebratory book.
Also thanks to our researcher, Carolyn Pogue
Czarnecki, and graphic designer, Bob Young.

Enlargements of all photographs in this book are
available through the Dene Nation office in Yellowknife.

Distributed in Canada, except to the Northwest
Territories, by McClelland and Stewart Limited.

Printed and bound in Canada
by D. W. Friesen & Sons Ltd.

Foreword

The Dene Nation, our nation of people, is at least thirty thousand years old. After a certain age you stop counting the exact years, and celebrating each one as they pass by.

Yet this book is a celebration. It is a celebration that a culture as old as ours is still thriving and evolving today. And it is a celebration that we, as a people, are rejuvenated with new strength and spirit, and are re-writing our modern-day history.

We are at a turning point. The push for industrial development has come to what some people know as the Mackenzie Valley. We call it Denendeh. It is our homeland. It is our background. We have chosen not to hide in our houses, curtain drawn, frightened, out of control.

Fifteen years ago we formed a central organization, and ever since, we have been struggling to prove that we are equal and valuable yet unique partners within Canada. Our Dene Nation has become an important political force in the North, and a strong ally to other aboriginal people across Canada.

This fifteenth anniversary celebration is to commemorate the great steps forward we have made in gaining recognition of our rights as an aboriginal nation; in preserving the richness and wisdom of our past; and in ensuring the strength and vitality of our future.

We are proud to present "Denendeh — A Dene Celebration". It is an important record of the Dene heritage, and an important milestone along the path we are clearing for our children. No human being would allow anyone else to suggest they are worthless, that they have no values worth passing on to others. All people have a desire for continuity of themselves in the future. That is why people have families, so they can pass on to their children their values and their own way of relating to the world.

For all of us in the North, this book may help prepare for the future by bridging the gaps between our different political, economic, and cultural traditions with increasing respect.

For people elsewhere, the book may help you understand that the North is more than bears, big fish, northern lights, and beautiful flowers. It is people, determined to be recognized and respected.

We hope this book will help you join in our celebration. We are tens of thousands years old. We are the first people of Canada. Perhaps it is time you got to know us better.

Welcome to Denendeh.

STEPHEN KAKFWI
Dene Nation president.

We the Dene

The word "Dene" is at the same time so rich and so simple that it means any human being, male or female, an individual or a group.

Over Thousands of Years

The aboriginal people of Canada form many linguistic groups. One of these, the Athapaskan family, is spread across Canada from the Shịh káedénila (Rocky Mountains) to Hudson Bay and far into the south-western United States. We, the Dene, belong to this family. We call our land, *Denendeh,* which means "The Land of the People." It is also known as the western part of the Northwest Territories and covers a vast area of 1,000,000 square kilometres.

This land, consisting of mountains, tundra and forests, has supported us, and the climate dictates that our people must be wily and strong, innovative and resourceful. Centuries of experience have given us intimate knowledge of our land and of her resources. We believe our land is a living person, often called "Mother", and we love her as we would a most generous parent. This feeling was expressed by Isidore Kochon of K'áhbamịtúé (Colville Lake):

"This land fed us all even before the time the white people ever came to the North. To us she is just like a mother that brought her children up . . ."

Our land has also been like a history book to us as every hill, creek, lake, bay, and peninsula has a Dene name indicating an event that has happened in that particular place. For example William Nerysoo of Teetl'it Zheh (Fort McPherson) tells the story of a creek which has its source in the plateau separating the Teetl'it Gwinjik (Peel) and Tsiigehnjig (Arctic Red River) watersheds and is known in English as Starvation Creek. We call it "again people coming together creek" or *chan łigaljil tshik.* The mouth of this creek does not freeze during the winter months and it is said that fish or *loche* can always be found

On the shore of Great Slave lake, two young Dene celebrate the beauty of their country.

7

there. In former years the Teetl'it Gwinjik (Peel River) people knew that they could always return to this creek in the event of a scarcity of game.

Another creek, named Paddle Creek in English, is called *taaʔaii khanjilnaii* in Loucheux. The name means "paddle it split apart" and derives from a small band of Inuit who penetrated far south into the heartland of Teetl'it Gwinjik (Peel River) country. It is said that by the time the Inuit had travelled up river for such a distance, they were forced to stop at this creek and fashion new paddles, their old ones having been broken up after a lengthy and difficult journey.

We have many such legends about the names we have given to places within Denendeh and each gives us a more intimate knowledge about our land and history.

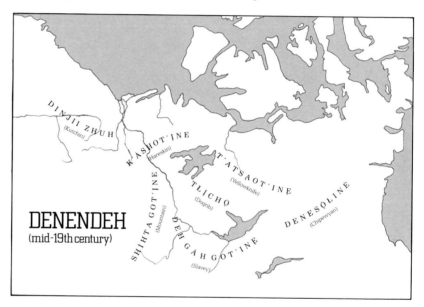

Before even the white people came or even since the white people came, when people were making their living trapping and hunting, although the boundaries are not written on maps and not drawn out on maps, the people from each community realize and respect other people's areas; although they are not written, although they are not drawn on the maps, they have respect for each other's areas, but when it comes to helping each other it does not matter, they help each other.

CHIEF DANIEL SONFRERE

The Bear River has the clearest water of any northern stream. In June, the winter ice still clings to the banks of the river.

Geographical conditions in Denendeh have created the groups of people who comprise the Dene Nation — Denesółiné (Chipewyan), Tłįchǫ (Dogrib), Deh Gáh Got'iné (Slavey), K'áshot'iné (Hareskin), and Dinjii Zhuh (Loucheux).

Denesółiné (Chipewyan), the largest group, have the reputation of being the most aggressive tribe. They have occupied the largest territory, hunting from Coronation Gulf and the Arctic Coast to Hudson Bay and all over the barren lands, as well as the subarctic forest. Caribou provided their major source of food, clothing and shelter. T'atsąot'iné (Yellowknives), a regional group, were also known as "Copper Indians" in historical documents because of the copper tools they used and traded.

Tłįchǫ (Dogrib) have lived between the Sahtú (Great Bear) and Tucho (Great Slave) lakes. They, too, have hunted the great caribou herds but an additional food source for them was fish from the lakes and rivers. Today, Tłįchǫ (Dogrib) live mainly in and around Bèhchokǫ̀ (Rae-Edzo), the largest Dene settlement with a population of approximately 1400.

Deh Gáh Got'iné (Slavey) traditionally have lived in the area south and west of Tucho (Great Slave Lake) and along Dehcho (Mackenzie River) and Nachaá Déhé (Liard River), and in the

mountains to the west of Dehcho Valley. Their language consists of a number of dialects, which are understood by most Dene today. In modern local usage, the English name Slavey applies also to K'áshot'įne (Hareskin), Sahtú Got'įne (Bearlake) and Shíhta Got'ine (Mountain) people. Deh Gáh Got'ine (Slavey) have relied on moose, woodland caribou, fish, birds, and small game for food.

K'áshot'įne (Hareskin) have lived west and northwest of Sahtú (Great Bear Lake), and besides caribou and moose, they have relied heavily on the Arctic hare for food and at one time for clothing. The hides of the hare were cut into strips and woven into warm clothing and blankets. Reincarnation was, and to some extent still is, an integral part of their religious beliefs. K'áshot'įne (Hareskin) are most closely related to Shíhta Got'įne (Mountain people), both linguistically and through intermarriage. Their main community is Rádeḷį Kǫ́ (Fort Good Hope).

Shíhta Got'įne (Mountain People), once lived between Dehcho and the Shíh Káedénila (Rocky Mountains), but today are mainly in Rádeḷį Kǫ́ (Fort Good Hope) and Tulít'a (Fort Norman). They are famous for their song-making and dances, and are well-respected for their great medicine powers. While most of the Dene relied on spruce or birch bark canoes, the Shíhta Got'įne are best known for the invention and use of the moose skin boat which was especially suited to the shallow waters of the Begá Dé (Keele), and other mountain rivers because the hide slipped easily over rocks and sand bars.

Sahtú Got'įne (Bearlake People) are descendants of the Deh Gáh Got'įne (Slavey), Tłįchǫ (Dogrib) and K'áshot'įne (Hareskin). They now live principally in the Délįne (Fort Franklin) and Sahtú (Great Bear Lake) areas. They, too, have depended on game and fish.

The Dinjii Zhuh (Loucheux) have enjoyed a varied lifestyle from the Richardson Mountains to the Chu Choo (Beaufort Sea). They are the most northern group of the Dene Nation and their language is significantly different from other Dene languages. They have had the most contact with the Inuit in the delta of the Dehcho (Mackenzie River), and shared the practice of tattooing with their northern neighbours. They are particularly noted for their finely crafted snowshoes, handicrafts, decorative motifs, and fancy clothing as well as being credited, along with the Shíhta Got'įne (Mountain People), for the invention of the moose skin boat. The Dinjii Zhuh (Loucheux) now live in the areas of Inuvik, Aklavik, Teetl'it Zheh (Fort McPherson), and Tsiigehtshik (Arctic Red River). Many also live in Van Tat Gwitch'in (Old Crow), the Yukon, and in Alaska.

Some Cree people live in Denendeh, especially around Tthebachaghé (Fort Smith) and Kátl'o Dehé (Hay River), and they are recognized as members of the Dene Nation. They are descendants of people who moved northward into the boreal forest of northern Alberta in the late 1780s to avoid smallpox. They have retained their language which is of Algonquin origin, but many of them also speak Denesǫ́łin Yaki (Chipewyan).

CREATION

When heaven's servants had made the earth, they took something resembling the hide of a large moose which was soft to the touch, and they spread it over the earth's surface.

Then they lifted it up again and the earth had become more beautiful.

Six times they repeated this process and that was how the world was made so beautiful.

My mother used to tell me that heaven created the earth.

With the coming of the fur traders two hundred years ago, a new line of descendants was born — part Indian, part White. The French gave them the name Métis. Until recent times, the Métis have lived like our aboriginal ancestors, primarily as hunters, fishermen and trappers. Although the Métis have their own organizations, they are equal citizens of Denendeh and possess aboriginal rights. At the community level, the relationship between both groups of aboriginal people has been characterized by harmony, mutual assistance in times of need, and by a minimum of racial tension.

Together we of aboriginal descent constitute over fifty percent of the resident population of Dehcho Valley.

Although we may belong to different tribes, in most areas of our lives we have shared common practices and traditions. We have shared our spirituality, our culture, our mythology and legends, family traditions, laws, and our forms of government and economics.

Music and games were and are basically the same throughout Denendeh. Men still play variations of the "hand game" and drum dances or *Ti* and round dances are an intrinsic part of communal celebrations.

In family life, both boys and girls underwent formal rituals at puberty, which included, for the girls, removal from the camp for days or weeks, although this is no longer practised. A celebration is still held when a young boy kills his first caribou or moose. Traditionally, marriages were arranged by parents and immediate relatives but today, young people choose their own partners.

Extended families have been the basic unit of Dene society. Children are easily adopted between families and the sharing of food is strongly emphasized. Through a consensual process, each group recognizes a leader, usually an elder, who has the respect of all. This consensus form of government is the foundation of the Dene Nation. It ensures participation and responsibility in decision-making by everyone. Thus, the real power stays with the people rather than being delegated to one person or group.

Education for our children began very early in life, as Eleanor McNeill explained, "In those days they'd teach kids all kinds of things, even the smallest one. When the women would clean the moosehides they'd tell the kids to help them. That's why when you get big you know what to do."

Learning encompassed every aspect of daily life from how to get along with family and neighbours to survival skills. Today we still use many of the old ways in teaching our children. Respect and peace are shown to males by addressing them as brother, uncle or grandfather; to females by addressing them as sister, aunt or grandmother even if they are not related. Children must learn that everything is shared — all kinds of foods, any game killed. As the young take more responsibility, parents have the duty to talk to their children to explain the work that must be done and how these tasks may be done safely.

Not only parents are teachers; everyone takes part in the

education of children. Leaders in every group are teachers too. At some gatherings good leaders talk late into the night and most parents take their children with them to these meetings and they are encouraged to listen. Grandparents are expected to teach their grandchildren as well, thus old values and traditions are passed on to the younger generations. The most important part of a child's education is to learn to show love for his people.

We realize that people and culture change with time and influence from outside but as Cindy Kenny-Gilday from Fort Franklin has said ". . . to maintain a sense of identity, [we] must maintain threads of common fabric from the past through the present to create a future for our descendants." Bertha Allen, president of the Native Women's Association of the Northwest Territories has suggested that this is most effectively done by example:

"Have pride in who you are. Restore your culture for your children and grandchildren. Respect yourself, respect other peoples' values, treat others as you would like to be treated. Share with one another your values in life. It's up to us to keep the culture and teach our children our values."

While we believe we are all responsible for education, the women have traditionally been most active in teaching moral values to the young. Alice Abel from Dettah expresses this very well:

"In the past, and still today, the native languages and traditional aboriginal spiritual values that the women have taught to their young children are to respect their elders, to love, to be honest, sharing, and caring for and respecting the land which provided the means of survival of the people. These values are very important and it is our women who can keep them alive because they are the first educators of our children."

At the Berger Inquiry in 1975, and so many other times, we spoke of our concern for the future of our young people. We criticized the practice of removing children from their families and communities in order to send them to residential schools. While it is important that young Dene receive training to allow them to compete successfully in the modern world, Lawrence Norbert of Tsiigehtshik (Arctic Red River) suggested that we must start building our own schools to train our people to be doctors, nurses, and teachers. "Who knows," he said, "they might even be prime ministers." But for those who do not desire to get an advanced academic education, the opportunity must be given to trap, hunt, and fish, and "experience the way of their . . . forefathers, with the thoughts and freedom and joy of being close to the earth and living on the land."

In the occupations of hunting and trapping and fishing, the learning process lasts a lifetime. As John Tetso, a Deh Gáh Got'i (Slavey) trapper and the first Dene to have a book published,

explained in his book, *Trapping is My Life:*

"In winter, with snow on the ground, trees and animal tracks can be used as a means of telling different kinds of country. Certain trees grow in certain places suited to them. A long line of big, tall spruce means a river, while the scraggy kind means muskeg. Poplars grow only on good hard ground. All these observations I have put to good use when hunting alone. My close observation of animals, too, comes in handy sometimes. The amphibious mink will travel along rivers, while the rambling marten prefers hills and high country. Caribou will travel on frozen muskeg in light snow, but as the snow gets deep it will retire to some hillside.

"All this and many more I have learned the hard way. It took years to accumulate all this knowledge about the bush life. Big things and little things."

In 1825, Robert McVicar of the trading company at Denínu (Fort Resolution), despaired of the Indians of that area ever becoming trappers for his company. He wrote:

"The most serious and lasting obstacle to the profitable employment of the resources of this district (furs) is the vicinity of the reindeer [caribou] . . . The abundance in which the Indians live, whilst on their lands, the small labour and skill required in hunting the reindeer, and the very clothing the skins of these animals afford, render the Chipewyans fond of revisiting thither . . . and to live independently of European supplies."

Denendeh was teeming with wildlife and we had learned to make use of her resources for our survival but not to accumulate personal wealth. McVicar wrote in his report the following year:

"A few of the Indians who came last spring from Fort Chipewyan on one or two occasions observed that their forefathers lived well and happy on their lands before the white man came among them, and they could still do the same."

The Tradition of the Drum

Our spirituality has sustained us for centuries and although it has taken different forms of expression among the Dene several aspects have remained the same, such as the drum and the power of "medicine".

George Blondin of Déline (Fort Franklin) explained:

"The tradition of the Drum has been going on for many years, before the non-Dene came into our country. The old people tell me that the Creator gave our people medicine powers to help them survive the hardships of living. It was part of religion. All people did not have the same kind of powers. Some individuals had very strong medicine

power, and to some a Drum Song was given. It's known that three or four of these special people existed in every tribe. Our people had some songs just for fun and dancing, but the sacred Drum Songs were used for praying, for healing, for seeing into the future.

"Life was so hard in the old days, people depended on the Drum Songs. They prayed to the Creator through the Drum Songs. Some of the songs are thanksgiving songs to the Creator when the people gather together after they've been apart all winter.

"Spiritual songs came from different areas and people learned them from each other. There are also different ways that people got their songs, through visions or through their medicine power.

"For example, there was a certain man who had a vision in which four drums appeared in front of him. No one was holding those drums, yet it was just like someone was singing. The man knew that this was meant for him so he didn't have to learn it. He just sang the song, words and all. It had lots of power. This particular drum song was a preaching song. The words went something like this:

> 'My people, the time on this earth is very short. So be good people, help each other. You have to work hard for a living. That's part of the order of our Creator. But don't complain. Love each other. Listen to this Drum Song and live by it. If you do this, you will see the promised land.'

"There was another special man who could look into the future with the drum. He would hit the drum and then he would predict important things that would happen. Because of the powers he possessed, the people had great respect for this man, people were good in that area of the land.

"Another medicine man lived in the Yukon, close to the Northwest Territories border. This man carried his drum in a white bag with a special design painted on it wherever he went. He really took care of that drum, just like it was a part of his body. He used the drum to preach. When he would hit his drum and sing, he would attract a lot of people.

"There is another man who had good influence on the people in his area. Nobody knew how he came to possess the wisdom that he had. Often a family would beg him to hit the drum for their children so that they would have good luck in the future.

"People often depended on their medicine people for helping them when they were sick or in trouble.

"We all know that in the early days, the Dene kept moving around following the game. But every summer they would have a gathering of all the people. That's when they would have a big Ti Dance. At that time their medicine people would sing prayer songs. They would concentrate and ask the Creator for what the people needed. They

OUR DRUM

The sun is the drum
That the Dene play
Music in the ripples
     across singing rivers

The wind is our hair
That blows
     through tall trees

Where is our song
But in the promise
     of tomorrow
Where is our heart
But in Denendeh

Our dance
Is life itself

ANTOINE MOUNTAIN

would start walking slowly in a circle as they sang and the crowd followed. Everyone sang, and in doing that, they were praying too. They would do a couple of rounds and stop, and then start a different song. Some songs were for thanksgiving, some were to have good luck and good health. After the prayers, the social part of the Ti Dance, just to have a good time, would begin. This was the proper traditional way to conduct a Ti Dance in the old days.

Dene Government

Although our leaders are very important to us, they are meant to guide us and not to have power over us. This is traditional among the Dene. As in the old days certain behavior is expected of those whom we choose to lead us and the rules are very clear. Leaders have been given special responsibilities by the Dene to lead, not assume dictatorial powers. It is the responsibility of leaders to have dialogue and debate issues, concerns, and laws with the people before formal decisions are made.

It is also the responsibility of our leaders of the Dene, to take positions on issues and concerns important to our people. Leaders must speak for themselves unless the people have a collective agreement on any given subject.

Government to be democratic can happen only through a sharing of power between people and leaders. Although decisions for the community are made by consensus, people are encouraged to make their own decisions about their personal lives. For example, at one meeting one Dene asked, "You, the leaders, where are you going to lead us?" And one leader answered, "We won't lead you anywhere . . . A Dene leader doesn't lead anybody anywhere. You go where you want to go."

All our assemblies are similar but different. People start slowly, letting their thoughts collect, listening, trying to understand, fighting off dependency, figuring out how things got to be this way. The elders, women and men, guide and question, providing the tools for the young people to use.

There is always prayer, a deeply religious blend of Christianity and Native spirituality. The drums play a big part and we are reminded that the "Creator owns the land and no one, no, not even the government, can change that."

The Dene way is very democratic because we talk things out until everyone agrees and there must be patience and respect for one another to do this. Under the struggle for consensus is the principle that we are all one and the circle must not break. It is often hard for a non-Dene to understand because the meetings start so slowly. The rules of order depend on good manners and respect. No one challenges anyone. Everyone has a chance to save face.

At the conclusion of a meeting in Tthebatthié (Fort Fitzgerald) in 1977, Jerry Antoine expressed to the old people

the feelings of all the youths present:

"We the young Dene are the future people who will continue the direction we will all take after this assembly is over. We are young. We are learning, and I would like to say to the elders that we . . . want your help. We want to help you in this whole struggle for self-determination. You are our elders. We are your children. You were children of your elders. We will not change our values. We may change like you have changed from your elders, but we will still be your flesh and blood. We will think like you. We respect you for being our elders. You are part of us and we are part of you."

Newcomers to Our Land

For thousands of years our ancestors lived according to our ways, undisturbed until the coming of the Europeans. In 1789, a dozen Dene guided Alexander Mackenzie down and up our great river, Dehcho. Stephen Kakfwi told the 1975 Berger Inquiry about this event:

"My people probably wondered at this strange pale man in his ridiculous clothes, asking about some great waters he was searching for. We never understand why our river is named for such an insignificant fellow."

More white people came to Denendeh, explorers, fur traders and missionaries, who built homes, trading posts, churches, and schools. Often this caused problems for our people as two very different cultures found themselves living side by side not always understanding each other. Stephen Kakfwi explained:

"When non-Dene came to our land, we saw them as curious strangers who had come to visit; we shared with them and helped them to survive. We could not conceive that they would not see the world as we do. We trusted what people said, for that was the way we had lived amongst ourselves. The Dene had no experience or understanding of a people who would try to control us, or who would say that somehow they owned the land we had always lived on."

In the late 1890s a few hundred prospectors also drifted down Dehcho on their way to the Klondike gold fields. Many, discouraged, forgot their golden dreams, and remained in Denendeh. The acceptance of the white people by the Dene was natural. During a court testimony in 1973 an old Dene, Antoine Beaulieu, was asked if the Dene did not like the coming of more white people in 1900. He replied, "We didn't mind. We didn't suppose they would bother us."

In 1899 the Canadian government proposed the signing of Indian Treaty Number 8 in order to keep the peace in a vast area which is now part of the Northwest Territories, Alberta, British Columbia and Saskatchewan. In 1900, the treaty party arrived at Denínu (Fort Resolution) to meet with the Dene who lived on the south shore of Tucho (Great Slave Lake).

WHILE THE RIVER FLOWS

The old Indian sat down
and lit his pipe,
and saw his grandchildren go.
Where the White River flow,
He tries to call them back
but it's too late, too late.

They learned too much
and forgot too much,
And he wonders if it will
ever be the same
With tears and sadness in his eyes.

JAMES CAESAR

NORTH DREAM OF MINE

North dream of mine
My father's too
You are us
And we are you
North mother take us
Back to your breast
All of our people
Into your nest
Northland love me
Teach me to know
Your graces and kindness
Our nation can show.
North mother of ours
Call your children once more
Give us wisdom and courage
In this lonely war
Give us yesterday's vision
Give us warriors like you
Give us words from old magic
And pride to renew

JAMES WAH-SHEE

Treaty Number 8 officially recognized that we are a nation and that we have aboriginal rights but, at the same time, it tried to extinguish our rights over our homeland. Our ancestors and their chiefs understood that the treaty was to protect our way of life and to guarantee our control of our traditional land. Chief Drygeese of the Tłįchǫ (Dogrib) declared:

"My people will continue to live as they were before and no white man will change that. You will in the future want us to live like the white man does, and we do not want that. The people are happy as they are. If you try to change their way of life by treaty, you will destroy their happiness. There will be a bitter struggle between your people and my people."

In 1920, when oil was discovered near the Dene village of Tulít'a (Fort Norman), the Canadian government became interested in the Dehcho Valley. Treaty Commissioner Henry A. Conroy was sent to negotiate Indian Treaty Number 11 with the Dene, but at the same time, he had been ordered not to change any word in the text of the treaty which he brought prepared from Ottawa. In every village we asserted our rights to control our resources and our land. Ted Trindell, a Métis from Łíídlį Kǫ́ę́ (Fort Simpson) who was present at the negotiations, testified:

"They talked about the land, and the Indians were scared that by taking treaty they would lose all their rights, but the Indians were told they would not. But if they were taking treaty they would still be free to roam and hunt as usual. No interference."

However, neither Treaty 8 nor Treaty 11 did protect our rights, and the 1920s and 1930s were decades of desperation for the Dene. The new territorial administration, established by Ottawa in 1921, passed game laws that brought hardships and resentment to the Dene. Illnesses, new to the Dene, such as measles, tuberculosis, and flu, took the lives of many people which included most of the leaders and elders. In 1928 one sixth of the Dene population died in a flu epidemic. During the great depression, hundreds of people fleeing the drought-ridden prairies and soup kitchens of the cities, came to our land, becoming summer prospectors and winter trappers. This, too, intensified problems for the Dene as there were clashes of culture as well as disputes over trapping methods. The Dene usually set only a few traps but these newcomers set up to five hundred traps and the small game population was greatly reduced.

In 1937, the Dene of Denínu (Fort Resolution), Bèhchokò (Fort Rae), Deschaghé (Rocher River) Łútsëlk'e (Snowdrift), and Sòmbak'è (Yellowknife), boycotted the annual visit of the Indian agent. The issue was not new — previously a head man had told the agent:

"Do you remember what you promised us before? . . . The time they began the treaty, they kissed the Bible and

everything. Why do you lie to us? Why do you do this? Why do you change now? You gave us paper and money; now you want to change the law. We will give you back all the money. We can do without the money. We did without it long before; you can't pay to be the boss of us . . . Why do you tell us how to run our land? We did not give it to you."

As a child,
I understood
How to give.
I have forgotten
This grace
Since I became
Civilized.

In 1941, when much of the world had been at war for two years, the Japanese bombed Pearl Harbour in Hawaii. Although far away from our land, that action began a chain of events that passed right through the heart of Denendeh and caused the little village of Tłegǫ́hłi (Norman Wells) to be regarded as an important military installation. The Americans feared that the Japanese might invade North America by way of Alaska. In preparation for the defense, 2,000 American soldiers, with tons of building supplies and heavy equipment, arrived in Denendeh in 1942. Their task was to make their way through bush, muskeg, lakes, and rivers, to Tłegǫ́hłi (Norman Wells) and construct a pipeline from there to Whitehorse in the Yukon. The effects of the three-year undertaking were traumatic for us and our land. The Americans left in 1945 but forty years later, debris still litters the land and many of us bear in our hearts other scars of this invasion. Amelia Gratix from Tthebachaghé (Fort Smith) described this time:

"We were very shocked to find ourselves one day with a whole army descended on us. We were unprepared. Our way of life changed drastically. The disruption of people's lives lasts forever. When I was only 25 years old, the U.S. army came to call . . . You see, when there's not enough single girls to go around they start with married women with all kinds of promises, maybe they buy things for them with money that their husbands don't have and the women get carried away with that kind of behaviour. They don't know that these are just short-lived things. Maybe they didn't have much before but it was more lasting . . . the soldiers left a bunch of pregnant girlfriends, women and children when they took their leave. You see, a marriage was something solid; the day you got married, that was it, as long as you lived. That was very abused afterwards . . . Life for the children was mixed up. They didn't know who their natural fathers were. The mothers absolutely refused to talk about it."

When exploration for oil and gas began in the Dehcho Valley in the mid 1950s, the Canadian government remembered that we still had aboriginal rights. In 1959, the Nelson Commission was established with the mandate "to inquire into the un-fulfilled promises of the Indian Treaties 8 and 11", particularly the allocation of Indian reserves. It was hoped that creating reserves would extinguish all our rights over our homeland. In some villages the people refused to listen to the commission members. "We know our situation is not good," they said, "but every time we accept a new deal from the Government, it gets worse."

The Nelson Commission report did not favor the formation of reserves. It recommended that the Dene be offered the following:

(a) title in fee simple to the plots of land on which they now reside . . .

(b) a cash settlement of $20 per acre for each acre to which the Indians of the Mackenzie District are entitled under the terms of Treaties 8 and 11 . . .

(c) an annual payment of one half of one per cent of any revenues derived by the Crown from the minerals, gas and oil resources of that portion of the Northwest Territories described in Treaties 8 and 11.

Neither the government nor the Dene wanted to see these proposals initiated and no more was heard from the Nelson Commission.

In 1967, Canada celebrated her hundredth birthday. The Northwest Territories received, as its gift, a new capital, Sòmbak'è (Yellowknife) and a northern-based administration; that is, Stuart Hodgson, federally appointed commissioner of the Northwest Territories, and his staff moved from Ottawa to Sòmbak'è (Yellowknife). Throughout the summer, communities were brought together to celebrate the centennial and we used this time for sharing our common hopes and problems.

Although we were the majority population in Denendeh, we were finding ourselves to have less say in the administration and laws of our land. Every year more mines were discovered and opened, roads were built, parks proposed, oil and gas wells drilled without our consent or often our knowledge. The education system in the territories provided no room for people who were different. Our children were being taken away for the purpose of education, and were returned to us years later as strangers to their own land, culture, and families.

In the mid 1960s the regional director of Indian Affairs, besides visiting individual communities, gathered the Dene chiefs in Tthebachaghé (Fort Smith) for a yearly advisory council meeting. More and more, these meetings proved to be exercises in frustration. As one of the chiefs later reported:

"We Indians were called out each year and told that the government people were wanting to hear what we thought, but I don't think they ever really listened. It was nice meeting and we got to see the Chiefs from other bands at the advisory council meetings, but we all felt the same, that we were the only ones who wanted to get things changed. Each year we went home and we would be back saying the same things again next year."

In October 1968 these meetings were abandoned forever. One of the reasons was that the new territorial administration was then supposed to provide all services to the Dene, and the Department of Indian Affairs was to shut its regional office in Tthebachaghé (Fort Smith), and to accept no more responsibility for treaty Dene.

We Have to Do it Ourselves

Our patience has endured for over a century, but by the late 1960s, clouds of discontent hung all over Denendeh. We came to the realization that patience was not enough if we were to survive as a nation and as a distinct people. The only answer to our increasing loss of control over our own lives seemed to lie in organizing ourselves, politically and economically.

In the early 1960s, the co-operative movement had reached the Dene after proving its worth in many Inuit communities. The Great Bear Co-operative was founded in Déline (Fort Franklin) marketing fish and handicrafts, operating a grocery store as well as providing other community services. The Denínu (Fort Resolution) Co-operative, formed in 1964, ran a sawmill and store. In 1965, the Etsaredi Co-operative in Bèhchokò (Fort Rae) organized group purchasing, domestic fishing, firewood cutting, municipal services, and the construction of a community hall.

While the government started to increase its power in our land and communities, we were not invited to take part in the decision-making process. The co-operatives, though not huge financial successes, helped us to retain some control over our lives as well as teaching us to analyze our situation and to organize. These experiences led us into more efficient political involvement later on. An atmosphere of hope and confidence began to permeate our meetings and our communities and we started to take positive steps to improve things in Denendeh.

In Tthebachaghé (Fort Smith) in March 1967, Thebacha Association was organized to promote leadership and economic opportunities and to help Native people take a more active role in society. Frank Laviolette and Chief Ed Bird spearheaded the movement and Harry Leishman, the executive secretary of the Indian-Eskimo Association, provided valuable assistance. Eddie Bellerose became the first Native to be hired as a community development officer.

The following year, the Deninoo Association was formed in Denínu (Fort Resolution) with similar goals and Jim Villeneuve was elected interim chairperson. A Dene craft store, Enekạ Kuẹ, was also opened.

A similar association, Sunrise, was organized in Kátl'o Dehé (Hay River) in 1969 to help people find housing, hold meetings about alcohol problems and open a friendship centre.

The Dene revival took many forms; political awareness, pride in cultural and traditional values, and spiritual renewal. Traditionally, "prophets" were wise men who possessed special spiritual powers and were able to help others find answers to troubling problems. Some of these prophets have been very influential in our history. In 1967, Joseph Pierre, a Slavey prophet from Indian Cabins in northern Alberta visited the southern part of Denendeh. This was the revival of the prophetic movement in Sòmbak'è (Yellowknife) and Bèhchokò (Fort Rae). From there it reached many Dene communities.

In June 1970, a new organization, the Tree of Peace, opened a

friendship centre in Sòmbak'è (Yellowknife). It provided space for cultural events, a kindergarten, an adult education centre, a film hall, and a meeting place for the band council. As well, community services such as bazaars, bingos, and fund raising events were held there. It housed the start of a library and was used as a resource centre. The *Native Press* reported:

"The kindergarten kids were surprised when their teacher at the beginning of the year, told them to sit down in Dogrib language. One little guy went home that night and told his mother, 'She told me to sit down in Dogrib.'"

A long time ago there were not any white people around our country then and not many problems so we didn't worry about our children. But now all the older people are worried very much about their children. Because there are many alcohol problems, and we don't know what is going to happen to our children.

Now we hear about pipeline and highway and Bear River dam — these things make us more worried than before. Of course they are on our land so we have to think hard and talk about it. This make us feel bad.

This is the way I feel about this. Maybe the other People they think the same way too.

Sample of written Slavey language by Dora Gully of Fort Franklin. The translation of this text is above.

This organization also arranged to broadcast forty children's programs in Slavey and English and twenty radio dramas in Slavey on CBC-CFYK in Sòmbak'è (Yellowknife). By August of that year, Tłįchǫ Yati (Dogrib) and Deh Gáh Got'įne zhatié (Slavey) language programs were underway and by 1972, Chipewyan was also being broadcast on the CBC.

In July 1970, the Tree of Peace arranged for thirty-three Dene to attend the annual Indian Ecumenical Conference, held for the first time on the Stoney Reserve near Morley, Alberta. Similar ecumenical conferences have been attended by the Dene every year since.

In 1967, we saw for the first time the written texts of Treaties 8 and 11 and heard them translated into our own languages.

When Chief Vital Bonnetrouge of Zhahti Kǫ́ę́ (Fort Providence) was told that the treaty provided for a one hundred square mile reserve for his band, he understood it to mean an allocation of one hundred miles by one hundred miles. He and other Dene leaders had been opposed to the establishment of reserves; now their opposition was strengthened when they realized how small it would be — ten miles by ten miles!

In January 1968, Louis Rabesca of Bèhchokǫ̀ (Fort Rae) began to collect recordings of the Bèhchokǫ̀ (Fort Rae) and Zhahti Kǫ́ę́ (Fort Providence) Dene who had been present at the signing of Treaty 11. In this work he was assisted by three members of the Company of Young Canadians. Other Dene joined the CYC: Charlie Charlo, James Wah-Shee, and Mike Canadien.

However, in July 1968, the regional director of Indian Affairs, during his annual visit to the Dene communities, once more "greeted the Chiefs and said that his boss in Ottawa had asked him to explain to the people the treaty signed in 1921." In Bèhchokǫ̀ (Fort Rae) the Dogribs and their chief Jimmy Bruneau boycotted the annual treaty ceremony until government officials recognized that they had never given up their land and that the treaties were only peace treaties.

In July 1968, the Department of Indian Affairs organized a three day Indian Act consultation meeting in Sòmbak'è (Yellowknife). Seven officials of the department attended, as well as eleven Dene, members of the Regional Indian Advisory Council, and one spokesman from each of the fourteen Indian bands. Mrs. Madeline Gibot of Tthebachaghé (Fort Smith) "considerably enlivened the session" when she lashed out at government policies and motives, past and present. She pointed out that "the Indians should not be afraid of the government any longer", and that "the best thing to do would be to tell the government how to do things, and not let the government tell them."

Some younger Dene were present as spectators, and on the second day one of them, Leon Sambele of Zhahti Kǫ́ę́ (Fort Providence), having been invited to bring forward his views, made the suggestion that, "there should be a federation of all Indians in the Northwest Territories." Joe Squirrel, also of Zhahti Kǫ́ę́, agreed that "the Indians of the Northwest Territories needed some kind of formal organization." Another delegate mentioned, "that a closer liaison between all the bands in the Territories was needed."

Mrs. Agnes Casaway of Denínu (Fort Resolution) suggested that "the delegates had a lot of work to do and this was their first opportunity to get together . . . this was a special Indian meeting and they wanted to be alone." And so, three times during the next three days, the government people were asked to leave the meeting. At the final closed session, the Dene decided to form an association to resolve the treaty issues. Leon Sambele was chosen as chairman of the interim board. Sadly, he died in February 1969, and never saw the completion of the organization he had helped to form.

Some young Dene began travelling to various communities

to listen to their elders. One of these young men was James Wah-Shee who said:

"In those early days it really hurt me to see my people losing hope. We were almost at the end of our rope, and we were looking for one last, good, solid thing to come along . . . Everywhere I went I watched the pain in the eyes of the old leaders and the look of being lost in the eyes of the young ones.

The idea of a solid organization was being formed in Manitoba around this time, and we sent two men there . . . [Leon Sambele and Steve Iveson]. They came back with very good reports about it, and we all talked about it for a long time with the old Indian people . . . It seemed to mean a kind of hope . . ."

In January and February 1969, George Manuel, an Indian from British Columbia, and Maurice Goutier, O.M.I., conducted community leadership workshops in Łíidlį Kǫ́ę́ (Fort Simpson), Zhahti Kǫ́ę́ (Fort Providence), Denínu (Fort Resolution), Bèhchokǫ̀ (Fort Rae), and Tthebachaghé (Fort Smith). At a final workshop in Sòmbak'è (Yellowknife), delegates selected by their communities recommended that a steering committee be set up to establish an organization of the Native people in the north, to be called The Native Brotherhood of the Northwest Territories.

At the end of his visit George Manuel left this message with the Dene:

". . . all we can say is keep organizing into groups for different purposes . . . never give up . . . you have a right to control your future . . . you must gain a voice in politics, in the economic field and the social field of your communities. You will run into a lot of jealousy, a lot of opposition; but don't give up. And if ever you should fail, don't worry. It's not a real failure, because you still will have learned. So just try again."

The following May, in Tthebachaghé (Fort Smith), Harold Cardinal, president of the Indian Association of Alberta, and, at age 24, a nationally respected leader, addressed students, members of the Thebacha Association, and numerous residents and visitors. He said, "As Native people we have to realize that the only way we can get ahead is by taking things in our own hands."

The Indian Brotherhood of the Northwest Territories

In July 1969, Pierre Catholique, chief of the Dene band in Łútselk'e (Snowdrift), was called to Yellowknife for a meeting with government officials. Part way through the meeting he was sent back home after being told, "What we have to discuss tomorrow doesn't involve you." Later, the chief found out that

the discussion that was not supposed to concern him was about the creation of a national park in the best hunting grounds of the Łútselk'e Dene. When the chief voiced his anger loudly, Parks Canada sent a twenty-one-man delegation to Łútselk'e (Snowdrift) to present strong arguments in favor of the proposed park. Only then did the Dene learn that this park had been in the planning for ten years. The people were angry that they had not been consulted earlier but they learned a valuable lesson in negotiation. Pierre Catholique explained, "Never again will one chief sit down with many government people. From now on, if 21 government people come to a meeting, 21 Indian leaders must come and sit across the table from them. From now on, we the chiefs, must talk with the government only when we are all together."

Within a week, the Dogrib chiefs answered a call for unity, and meeting in Sòmbak'è (Yellowknife), they discussed again the idea of an Indian Brotherhood.

In October 1969, during a meeting of our sixteen chiefs, we formed the Indian Brotherhood of the Northwest Territories. Mona Jacob, a community worker for Thebacha Association was elected president and Neil Colin, Joe Catholique, Charlie Charlo, and Ray Sonfrere were elected vice-presidents. We wanted all descendants of the Dene to be members of our brotherhood, but the minister of Indian Affairs refused to recognize an organization that would include anyone classified by the government as "non-status" or "Métis".

In February 1970, all our chiefs ratified the Charter of our Brotherhood, and chose a provisional executive with Roy Daniels as President.

The Constitution of the Indian Brotherhood defined its objectives:

A. To uphold the rights and interests of the Indian People of the NWT, in reference to their treaties and otherwise.

B. To develop, discuss, and promote policies for the Indian People of the NWT.

C. To conduct, foster and support programs and policies

for the economic, social, educational, social health and cultural benefit of the Indian Peoples of the NWT.

D. To give voice to the opinions of the Peoples of the NWT.
E. To co-operate with other organizations of similar or friendly purpose.

After the first hectic year of the Indian Brotherhood, James Wah-Shee was elected president and remained in that position until 1975. An elderly Dogrib woman verbalized the hope that quickened among the people:

"They could ignore some of us, and beat some of us, and steal from some of us, and pat some of us on the head before, but they will never be able to do that to us again, because we have our Indian Brotherhood now."

With a similar vision, the Committee for Original Peoples' Entitlement, known as COPE, was officially founded in Inuvik in January 1970 to protect the interests of all Native people of the Mackenzie River delta, — Dene, Métis and Inuit. Agnes Semmler was the first president.

In August 1971, Oxfam approved a grant to the Indian-Eskimo Association of Canada to buy a Cessna 185 aircraft. Wally Firth began to fly into communities in the Yukon and Northwest Territories, helping native organizations and bringing them news of what was happening in other parts of Denendeh. There was much work to do. Our communities and bush camps are hundreds of kilometres apart, so communications became a priority.

Education in the Dene languages, for both children and adults, had a small beginning as we became more and more assertive. We recognized the need for action in all areas of life, but the primary goal for our new brotherhood, with limited time and limited funds, was to research and prove that the treaties had not abolished our sovereignty. Although we already knew this, we had to document it for the benefit of others.

In June 1969, the minister of Indian Affairs presented to Parliament "A Statement of the Government of Canada on Indian Policy," better known ironically, as The White Paper. In essence, the paper proposed the repeal of the Indian Act and the transfer of all responsibilities for Indians from the federal government to the provinces and territories. The White Paper sparked outrage among Indian people across Canada who were entitled to special status under the British North America Act. The Indian Association of Alberta answered in June 1970, with its own manifesto, "Citizens Plus".

Although the White Paper was officially withdrawn and generally not implemented across Canada, certain aspects of it were already in process in Denendeh. In 1955, all Northwest Territories schools had been transferred from the Indian Affairs branch to the territorial administration. Under Stuart Hodgson, the commissioner of the Northwest Territories since 1967, southern-style settlement or hamlet councils were

organized in each village, which proved to be harmful to our own political structures. This led us to further distrust the territorial government.

After the White Paper, the last representative of Indian Affairs was removed from Denendeh, and even the responsibility for distributing the annual treaty money was transferred to the government of the Northwest Territories. In 1971, the board of directors of the brotherhood asked the federal government "to correct the unconstitutional, illegal, and immoral practice of transferring federal responsibilities for Indian People to the Territorial Government of the NWT." In April 1972, the Department of Indian Affairs reopened an office in Sòmbak'è (Yellow-knife) but its representative didn't have as much power as his provincial counterparts.

The Caveat

At a meeting in Bèhchokǫ̀ (Fort Rae) in March 1973, the Dene chiefs decided to file a "caveat" in the Territorial Land Titles Office. The caveat was to be a legal declaration that we have aboriginal rights to all of Denendeh, and that no decision about our land could be taken by the Canadian government without our consent. Mr. Justice William Morrow of the Supreme Court of the Northwest Territories, spent the summer of 1973 travelling to all the Dene communities to hear the evidence of the old people regarding the treaties. At the hearings in Sòmbak'è (Yellowknife), anthropologists and legal experts also testified. By September he brought down his landmark decision which stated that the "indigenous people" were the owners of the land covered by the caveat and "that they have what is known as aboriginal rights . . ." He further stated that he doubted that aboriginal title to the land had ever been extinguished and that the caveators should be permitted to put forward a claim for title to the land. Judge Morrow also admonished the Canadian government that it had an obligation to protect the legal rights of the Native people.

Dene women of Rae line up on "Treaty Day" to receive the five dollar annuity, promised to each Dene by the 1921 treaty.

Later, the Court of Appeal and the Supreme Court of Canada overturned the right to apply for a caveat on a legal technicality, but the other decisions of Justice Morrow have never been challenged in court.

His judgement, plus the landmark decision of the Supreme Court of Canada recognizing aboriginal rights of the Nishga in 1973, forced the federal government to adopt a new policy towards Native peoples' rights. In January, 1974, the minister of Indian Affairs told the Northwest Territories Council that "the time has come to meet and deal with Native peoples' concerns, including claims . . . I am ready to negotiate immediately . . . There will be a settlement. And it will be a negotiated settlement of the claims of the Native peoples."

In 1969 the government had appointed an Indian Claims Commissioner for Canada, former territorial councillor, Dr. Lloyd Barber. Five years later, in a powerful and provocative speech to the Rotary Club in Sòmbak'è (Yellowknife), he said, in part:

". . . I cannot emphasize too strongly that we are in a new ball game. The old approaches are out. We've been allowed to delude ourselves for a long time because of a basic lack of political power in Native communities. This is no longer the case and there is no way that the newly emerging political and legal power of Native people is likely to diminish. We must face the situation squarely as a political fact of life but more importantly as a fundamental point of honour and fairness. We do, indeed, have a significant piece of unfinished business that lies at the foundations of this country."

We also were facing a lot of unfinished business. The Indian Brotherhood and the Métis Association, organized in 1973, joined forces, and held their first joint general assembly in June 1974, in Rádeḷi Kǫ́ (Fort Good Hope). Initially, land claims negotiations had been considered as leading towards settlements involving land grants and cash settlement. But the new theme for an agreement became "land, not money." Indian Brotherhood president James Wah-Shee argued:

". . . The Indian people are not seeking to sell their land for money, no matter how much! We are now the lawful owners of the land and we intend to remain owners of the land. Compensation in the way of money is but incidental."

In July 1975, the village of Łiidlį Kǫ́ę́ (Fort Simpson) on Dehcho was the setting for the second annual Joint General Assembly of the Indian Brotherhood and the Métis and Non-Status Association of the Northwest Territories. Over three hundred delegates voted unanimously to adopt the historic Dene Declaration.

The Dene Declaration

We the Dene of the N.W.T. insist on the right to be regarded by ourselves and the world as a nation.

Our struggle is for the recognition of the Dene Nation by the government and people of Canada and the peoples and governments of the world.

As once Europe was the exclusive homeland of the European peoples, Africa the exclusive homeland of the African peoples, the New World, North and South America, was the exclusive homeland of Aboriginal peoples of the New World, the Amerindian and the Inuit.

The New World like other parts of the world has suffered the experience of colonialism and imperialism. Other peoples have occupied the land — often with force — and foreign governments have imposed themselves on our people. Ancient civilizations and ways of life have been destroyed.

Colonialism and imperialism is now dead or dying. Recent years have witnessed the birth of new nations or rebirth of old nations out of the ashes of colonialism.

As Europe is the place where you will find European countries with European governments for European peoples, now also you will find in Africa and Asia the existence of African and Asian countries with African and Asian governments for the African and Asian peoples.

The African and Asian peoples — the peoples of the Third World — have fought for and won the right to self-determination, the right to recognition as distinct peoples and the recognition of themselves as nations.

But in the New World the Native peoples have not fared so well. Even in countries in South America where the Native peoples are the vast majority of the population there is not one country which has Amerindian government for the Amerindian peoples.

Nowhere in the New World have the Native peoples won the right to self-determination and the right to recognition by the world as a distinct people and as Nations.

While the Native people of Canada are a minority in their homeland, the Native people of the N.W.T., the Dene and the Inuit, are a majority of the population of the N.W.T.

The Dene find themselves as part of a country. That country is Canada. But the Government of Canada is not the government of the Dene. The Government of the N.W.T. is not the government of the Dene. These governments were not the choice of the Dene, they were imposed upon the Dene.

What we the Dene are struggling for is the recognition of the Dene Nation by the governments and peoples of the world.

And while there are realities we are forced to submit to, such as the existence of a country called Canada, we insist

Dene Nation poster.

Little People
Old and Young
Did it!

Little dreams
Big hopes
Did it!

A forgotten nation
That wants to be remembered
Did it!

Small tribes
Big Tribes
Together

One battle
Many battles
To win

A new faith
And new ways
And we'll win!

on the right to self-determination as a distinct people and the recognition of the Dene Nation.

We the Dene are part of the Fourth World. And as the peoples and Nations of the world have come to recognize the existence and rights of those peoples who make up the Third World the day must come and will come when the nations of the Fourth World will come to be recognized and respected. The challenge to the Dene and the world is to find the way for the recognition of the Dene Nation.

Our plea to the world is to help us in our struggle to find a place in the world community where we can exercise our right to self-determination as a distinct people and a nation.

What we seek then is independence and self-determination within the country of Canada. This is what we mean when we call for a just settlement for the Dene Nation.

Reaction to the Dene Declaration was predictable. There were rumours that political "radicals" were working with the Brotherhood and that the Dene were being trained in techniques of guerilla warfare. Although the rumours were unfounded, the RCMP employed undercover operatives to infiltrate the Brotherhood until 1978 when the police found that worries of Dene violence were unfounded.

The Dene Declaration heralded a new era of concern and support. George Manuel, now president of the National Indian Brotherhood said:

"It is hardly surprising that the indigenous people in Canada identify with the emerging countries of the Third World. We share the common experience of poverty; our lands and peoples have been exploited for the benefit of others; and like the people of the Third World, we are struggling for economic independence and self-reliance.

The Dene Declaration has given us hope . . . It subscribes to the principle that aboriginal rights must not be extinguished but preserved; that the settlement be one of land and political authority over the land — not cash compensations for extinguishment. In other words, what is required is a new political system giving a degree of political sovereignty to the Indian people never before experienced in this country."

Southern supporters grew in number, and throughout the following years, we received moral, financial, and political help from every province in Canada. Demonstrations, prayers, money, letters, and speeches gathered momentum as the years went on.

We believe our struggle came to symbolize the struggle of all people, in all walks of life, for control over their lives and for a more careful stewardship of the natural resources of this country.

In September 1975, a coalition of three major Canadian Christian churches, United, Roman Catholic and Anglican, formed "Project North". The purpose was to support northern aboriginal people in their struggle for justice and self-determination as well as challenging Christians and other people in southern Canada to become involved in the ethical issues of northern development. Later, the group was joined by Mennonite, Lutheran, Quaker, and Presbyterian churches and by the Canadian Religious Conference.

In spite of this good will and support, our troubles were far from over. The oil and gas companies were applying pressure to build a pipeline immediately in the face of protests from the Dene. The government was still not including us in decisions regarding our land. These problems, combined with tensions in the Brotherhood administration caused strife within the organization. At the general assembly in Bèhchokò (Fort Rae) in December 1975, James Wah-Shee resigned as president of the Indian Brotherhood. At this time, the minister of Indian Affairs demanded that a land claims proposal be in place by November 1, 1976, creating even more pressure on the troubled brotherhood.

For seven months, we worked with the acting president, Richard Nerysoo, of Teetl'it Zheh (Fort McPherson), to reduce the dissent in the painful internal struggle. At the Tulít'a (Fort Norman) general assembly in July 1976, the chiefs talked around the table for two days. Hugh McCullum of Project North described the scene:

"There was no dancing the first night. People stood around all night in the July sunlight in the dusty paths, talking earnestly in Dogrib and Loucheux, in Slavey and in Chip. The drums had been silent since the meeting in Fort Rae, the previous December — the only meeting the drums were not used.

"Election of the executives came late on the second day. Georges Erasmus became president, and George Barnaby, vice-president. Chiefs stood up then, announcing their support and making it unanimous. At one a.m., the Fort Rae drummers began to heat their caribou skin drums over a small wood fire outside the old community hall, down near the bank of the placid river. We danced all night. The drums would never be silent again; the throbbing heartbeat of a nation taking another step toward self-control.

"It was seven a.m. before we slipped away to our tents to sleep for a few hours before the assembly resumed its meetings. Earlier that evening a rain squall had briefly drenched the community and the two hundred delegates who were meeting to chart the future of the Dene Nation. But now, two enormous rainbows arched across the sky from the Franklin Mountains over the river into the purple hills to the west.

" 'The Creator is pleased', old Julian Yendo told his friends."

THEY SAY

The drummers put down their
drums
They started to sing and made a
circle
They kept on singing
and dancing
People came behind them
More people and more people

til the circle was very big

Everybody joined hands
locked arms
We held each other up
We faced each other
as we moved and sang
feeling our strength and power
Happy

They say
that in the old days
a long time ago
when the Dogribs and the
Chipewyans
came together to make peace
They say
the people danced like this
for three days

We danced for a long time
people of many ages
together
moving
with the power of
our own voices
and our own heartbeats.

Walking home
in the early morning
I could still hear the drum
far away

The circle of the Nation
circle of the people

In the old days
the people danced like this
for three days
they say.

M. HELENE LARAQUE

We were now ready for a general assembly to ratify the Agreement-in-Principle to be presented to the Canadian government before the November deadline.

But the road to the assembly was not smooth. A rift between the executives of the Indian Brotherhood and those of the Métis Association widened. In general, the Dene wanted their aboriginal rights recognized before construction of the Mackenzie Valley pipeline. But some Métis leaders proposed that construction and negotiation could take place simultaneously. Because of the rift, the government cut off all regular loans to the brotherhood and it appeared we would not be able to hold the assembly. But the Roman Catholic and Anglican churches decided to lend us the necessary money.

Warren Allmand became minister of Indian Affairs in September, 1976 and we were once again dealing with a new man. After our general assembly at Łíídlį Kǫ́ę́ (Fort Simpson) in early October, we went to Ottawa, and on October 25, presented to the minister our Agreement-in-Principle which outlined our concepts basic to future negotiations.

The Dene position was clear:

"We are not demanding extraordinary rights, though we are calling for a radical change in the historical relationship between aboriginal people and the people of Canada. It is because we believe that what we are demanding is nothing less than a universal human right that we have taken the unusual step of affirming our support for the rights of the non-Dene in our proposal. Furthermore, we see no reason why our right to self-determination cannot be met within Canadian Confederation."

However, as of 1984 the Agreement-in-Principle between the Dene and the Government of Canada has not been signed.

A Frontier to Exploit or a Homeland?
The Berger Inquiry.

Since the early 1970s, oil and gas companies had been planning to construct and operate a natural gas pipeline through Denendeh from the Arctic Coast to southern Canada and the United States. On March 10, 1971, the minister of Indian Affairs and Northern Development, told the Society of Petroleum Engineers in Dallas, Texas: "We in Canada would welcome the building of such a gas pipeline through our country and would do everything that is reasonable to facilitate this particular development". And on March 19, 1971, the environment minister expressed his optimism: "I am 90 percent certain that a Mackenzie Valley corridor containing not only two pipelines, but a highway and possibly a railway could be underway by 1973."

In fact, on April 28, 1972, Prime Minister Trudeau announced that the construction of a highway from Łiidlį Kǫ́ę́ (Fort Simpson) to Tuktoyaktuk would start that summer, to be completed

by 1976. "The route will be carefully selected for the use of any gas and oil pipeline . . ." He said further that the whole system would be of immense benefit for Canadians because "it would encourage the outflow of resources and the inflow of people."

In 1973, the government of Canada designated Mr. Justice Thomas Berger to inquire into the social, environmental, and economic impact the construction and operation of such a pipeline would have. For the first time, we felt the federal government was serious about listening to northern people at official public meetings.

Beginning in 1975, Berger travelled to twenty-six communities in the north, and to some cities in southern Canada. In the north alone, he listened to over 1,000 testimonies. We spoke through this patient judge to the government, to the citizens of Canada, and indeed to the world. Through radio and TV coverage, for the first time, we were able to hear news in our own languages the day it was made. Native broadcasters were Louis Blondin, Joe Tobie, Jim Sittichinli and Abe Ookpik. The inquiry lasted almost two years and had an enormous impact on thousands of Canadians — those who spoke and those who listened.

We had powerful things to say. Chief Frank T'Seleie of Rádełį Kǫ́ (Fort Good Hope) addressed the chairman of Foothills Pipe Lines:

"You are coming to destroy a people that have a history of 30,000 years. Why? For 20 years of gas? Are you really that insane? The original General Custer was exactly that insane. You still have a chance to learn. A chance to be remembered by history as something other than a fool bent on destroying everything he touched. You still have a chance, you still have a choice. You could destroy my nation . . . or you could be a great help to give us our freedom. Which choice do you make . . .? Which choice do you make for your children and mine?"

Up and down Dehcho Valley, Judge Berger heard testimonies similar to this, in English, Slavey, Dogrib, Loucheux, and Chipewyan. After twenty-one months of debates and presentations, Judge Berger declared at the last session on November 19, 1976:

"There is a kind of conventional wisdom that says a decision like this should only be made by the people in government and industry. They have the knowledge, they have the facts and they have the experience. Well, the hearings we have held show that the conventional wisdom is wrong . . .

". . . At this Inquiry we have tried to discover the true North. I say that because we have to understand the condition of the North today if we are going to be able to predict what the impact of the pipeline and the corridor will be . . .

"The future of the North is a matter that is important to us all. What happens here will tell us something about what kind of country Canada is, what kind of people we are."

"I was born in Fort Good Hope in 1953. When I was two years old my mother caught TB and was taken away. I was taken care of by the people of Fort Good Hope. The people there are like that. If a child doesn't have a mother, it is everybody's responsibility to make sure the child doesn't starve . . . The child is not taken off to some home, you know, to strangers either. I was kept by many families until my foster parents . . . learned about my situation . . . they were kind people and they knew that I needed help, so they adopted me.

. . . I was raised in Colville Lake. In the summer we lived in fish camps, always working together making dry fish, cutting wood, and I look back on those days as really happy. I was happy . . .

I look at Colville Lake today . . . (the people) still have their own lives, they still have their own pride. I don't want my people to have nothing but memories of what their life used to be. . ."

BELLA T'SELEIE

The Dene make a presentation to the Berger Inquiry, Yellowknife. April 1976.

Left to right:

Charlie Snowshoe, trapper; Freddie Greenland, chief of Aklavik; Betty Menicoche, fieldworker; Louis Blondin, interpreter; Wilson Pellissey, trapper; Phoebe Nahanni, director, land use and occupancy research.

In his report of April 15, 1977, Justice Berger recommended that a Mackenzie Valley pipeline, or any other major project in Dehcho Valley, should be postponed for ten years to allow sufficient time for Native land claims to be settled, for new programs and new institutions to be established, and for an orderly, not hasty, program of exploitation. He said:

"A Mackenzie Valley pipeline . . . if it were built now, . . . would bring limited economic benefits, its social impact would be devastating, and it would frustrate the goals of Native claims."

To some, the decision was a disappointment; to others, an outrage and a loss of potential fortunes. But to us, the Berger report was a victory in the sense that, finally, people from other parts of Canada were listening and beginning to understand what the Dene Nation was all about. Churches and labour movements, environmentalists and individuals heard and heeded. From Halifax to Victoria and back again, people held rallies, marches, church services, "Awareness Weeks," and hosted speaking tours in support of the Dene.

We Need To Tell the World Who We Are

Over six hundred Dene attended our national assembly in June 1977 at Tthebatthié (Fort Fitzgerald), the largest assembly to that date. There we decided not to distinguish between status, non-status, and Métis people because these divisions were created by non-Dene. All people of Native ancestry in Denendeh could declare themselves Dene and sign the "Declared Dene Registry."

In spring and summer 1977, the Dene Nation and Warren Allmand, then minister of Indian and Northern Affairs, held four negotiation sessions which proved to be very honest and fruitful. Allmand accepted "the concept of a land area which would be a Dene area for the Dene Nation, where there would be a government with power, and that area would be within Confederation."

In June 1977, Montreal citizens concerned about Northern development march in support of the Dene and of the recommendations of the Berger Report.

Allmand and the Dene came close to a settlement but in the fall, he was replaced as minister by Hugh Faulkner who proposed that "Indian reservations" be the basis for the settlement of Dene rights and separated the negotiations for political rights from the land ownership and compensation issues. We could not accept these terms and the result was a stalemate in negotiations that lasted until 1981.

On August 3, 1977, the Federal Government released a paper on "Political Development in the Northwest Territories", and Prime Minister Trudeau appointed Charles M. (Bud) Drury as his special representative for constitutional development in the Northwest Territories. We understood well the meaning of this document. In a press release we stated:

> ". . . The Cabinet document suggests that there is no relation between political rights and the survival of a culture. Such a statement is absurd . . . How can culture exist and grow without self-determination? . . . the Cabinet . . . endorses the view of the North as a frontier to be exploited, rather that a homeland . . ."

We decided not to participate in the Drury Inquiry. We felt that all relevant questions had been answered and discussed at the Berger Inquiry.

At the National Assembly held in March 1978 in Délįne (Fort Franklin), we once again solemnly proclaimed that we are one people. Chief Johnny Charlie stated:

> "The aboriginal people of the Mackenzie Valley are one and we reject the false divisions created by the Indian Act. We wish to admit to full membership all those descendants of the aboriginal people of the Mackenzie Valley who have declared themselves to be Dene."

During a three-hour, emotion-charged discussion, delegate after delegate expressed a desire for nationhood within the

At the Dene National Assembly in Fort Franklin in March 1978, the Dene demand to be recognized as the "Dene Nation".

Canadian context. By unanimous vote, we changed the name of our organization from "The Indian Brotherhood" to the "Dene Nation," in order to formally proclaim to all what we had always known — that we are a nation of people.

In her soft Slavey language, Stella Mendo of Tulít'a (Fort Norman) expressed this belief:

"... when we name our children we give them powerful names. Names that are strong. Our land is strong. Our people are strong and our people are one. We need a strong, powerful name to tell the world who we are. Let us call ourselves the Dene Nation."

When we asserted our nationhood in the small village of Déline (Fort Franklin), we did not realize that our definition of a nation paralleled the one accepted by the United Nations in 1977:

"All peoples have the right to self-determination. By virtue of that right they freely determine their political status and freely pursue their economic, social and cultural development ...

Two years after the proclamation of the Dene Nation, the Métis Declaration was passed by a joint Dene-Métis Assembly at Rádeli Kò (Fort Good Hope) and by the general assembly of the Métis Association, also in 1980.

We the Métis people of the Northwest Territories do declare that we exist as a national entity. While it is true that our nationalism does not take the form of a nation state, it is sufficient to define us as a distinctive people. While it is true that we are descendants of the Dene of the Northwest Territories, we are also descendants of other nationalities. As such we have evolved as a people that are distinct from both groups.

From the newcomers to Canada, we inherit democratic rights as citizens of the nation state that they have established. As such we declare ourselves as loyal citizens of Canada. From our Dene ancestors, we inherit legal rights that are owed to us by the nation state. As such we declare that we are possessed of the legal concept known as Aboriginal Rights.

Therefore we declare our desire to enter into negotiations with the Government of Canada to bring our Aboriginal Rights into a substantive form. We further declare that it is our desire that these negotiations should lead to our recognition as Métis people.

The Native Women's Association of the Northwest Territories was formed in July 1977, for all women of aboriginal descent including Métis and non-status Dene. The organization's aims "are to concentrate energy at the grassroot level." In their communities, the women wanted to improve conditions in "health, education, social services, and the provision of opportunities to increase self-sufficiency." Bertha Allen was elected president and is still in that position today. The women enthusiastically began projects to fulfill their objectives. A few of the many successes have been: the operation of an arts and crafts

Left:
At the Dene National Assembly in Fort Norman in 1978, Pat Bugghins of Hay River makes a plea for unity among the Dene. Herb Norwegian, of Fort Simpson, translates the Slavey language into English.

Left:
In 1980, Fort Good Hope, a community of 600, welcomes 550 Dene from all over Denendeh for the Dene National Assembly.

JOHN FARCY JR., FORT PROVIDENCE

retail outlet in Sòmbak'è (Yellowknife); two home management facilities in Sòmbak'è (Yellowknife) and Inuvik; pre-employment training to encourage women to get into the workforce; and development of a Native placement program to ensure that foster children go to Native homes.

We were now taking steps to regain control of all aspects of our lives. By September 1978, six Dene communities had voted to have alcohol prohibition and many had developed alcohol education programs. CBC radio is now broadcasting news and information programs in all Dene languages. The Native Communications Society, incorporated in 1974, took over publishing the popular *Native Press* newspaper every second week. By 1981 Slavey languages were being taught in the schools at Délįne (Fort Franklin), Rádelį Kǫ́ (Fort Good Hope), and Zhahti Kǫ́ę́ (Fort Providence). Dogrib, Chipewyan and Loucheux language school booklets have been published by the Department of Education.

William Nerysoo of Fort McPherson.

In April, 1979, Stuart Hodgson resigned his position as commissioner of the Northwest Territories. He commented, "My greatest sorrow is that I haven't been able to establish a good relationship with the Dene."

Since 1979, our chiefs and leaders have encouraged more active participation in the territorial government. In a press release we stated: "We do recognize territorial council as an important platform from which to fight for much needed changes to the exisiting system." In the territorial election of October 1979, a majority of Native people (Dene, Métis, and Inuit) were elected to the council, now known as the Legislative Assembly. Two Dene, Richard Nerysoo and James Wah-Shee, took charge of territorial government departments.

Although we were making gains as we implemented changes in our communities and formed organizations to improve so many facets of our lives, we still had other struggles facing us.

Frank Laviolette worked to establish and protect buffalo herds in Elk Island Park and Fort Providence Sanctuary.

In November 1980, Bill C-48, the oil and gas Act concerning the Northwest Territories and off-shore, was presented to the House of Commons. The bill gave the federal minister of energy exclusive control on all Canada's lands over oil and gas exploration, productivity, delivery, pricing, revenue sharing, and taxation. This bill meant we would have no say as to how these resources were exploited in Denendeh. We were not alone in our objection to this act as some people in southern Canada disapproved as well. Despite protest campaigns all over the country, the bill became law in December 1981.

Another concern we had to deal with was our disagreement with the government over the Canadian Constitution. We and all Native people in the country, wanted it to define and guarantee our aboriginal rights. After many representations to Ottawa and energetic lobbying by the Northwest Territories Legislative Assembly, a clause was included in Canada's constitution, passed on December 2, 1981 which reads: "The existing aboriginal and treaty rights of the aboriginal peoples of Canada are

Jim Balsillie of Fort Resolution.

Catherine Mitchel of Inuvik.

George Blondin of Fort Franklin.

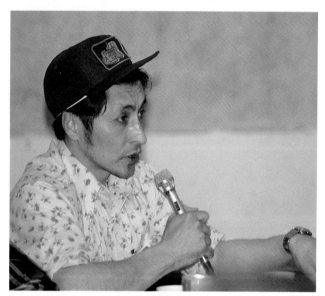

Freddie Greenland, chief of Aklavik.

Alexis Arrowmaker of Snare Lake,
former Chief of Rae Edzo.

John Bekale of Rae Lakes.

hereby recognized and affirmed." Although these rights have not been defined clearly, the statement represents to us a partial victory.

In February 1980, Esso Resources proposed expansion of the Norman Wells oil field and Interprovincial Pipe Lines proposed the construction of a pipeline from Tłegǫ́hłi (Norman Wells) to northern Alberta — a $400 million dollar project. The plan included building six artificial islands in Dehcho River. Structures such as these had never been built in a large river anywhere in the world. Naturally, we were concerned about what the impact would be on the environment and eco-system of the river by both these projects. The Dene Nation and the Métis Association actively opposed the plan.

In April 1981, the National Energy Board approved the recommendations of the Environmental Assessment Review Panel for the project but had to admit that, even if all technical problems were solved successfully, it was expected that smaller Native communities would "experience some increase in alcohol-related problems, heightened child welfare problems, an increase in criminal offence rates, and other social problems."

We issued a strong statement objecting to the projects going ahead without careful planning to prevent these problems from arising. We believed there could be some benefits to our people but we were convinced that proper ecological and social studies had not been done to prepare for the impact. Native and territorial government leaders met to discuss the ramifications,

National Energy Board hearings in Yellowknife, in 1980.
Left to right:
George Tuccaro, Rene Mercredi, Bob Stevenson.

both good and bad, of these projects and they presented a package of conditions which included: demands for resource revenue sharing, guaranteed energy supplies at a preferred price; joint planning; and meaningful progress on negotiations of aboriginal rights.

The aboriginal rights negotiations between the Dene and the federal government re-opened in July, and a day later, the Cabinet gave final approval for the building of the Tłegǫ́hłi (Norman Wells) pipeline. Feeling that this approval was too hasty, we left the negotitating table. A month later, the government promised to put a two year moratorium on the construction of the pipeline, and to give northerners over twenty million dollars to prepare for the impact. Although we still opposed the project it was clear it was going ahead anyway. We returned to negotiations and voted to accept some of the money to prepare our people for the pipeline and the oil field expansion.

We wanted the federal government to acknowledge our ownership rights to the Norman Wells oil resources so we would have some control over the project and share in the benefits. As this goal seemed temporarily unattainable, our leaders accepted to enter into partnership with Esso Resources for the ownership and operation of a drilling rig. This business structure known as "the joint venture" is so complicated that it couldn't be translated into our Dene languages and discussed in our traditional way.

In December 1983, Georges Erasmus, in his testimony to the Beaufort Sea Environmental Assessment Panel, voiced our deep disillusionment about most aspects of the Norman Wells project:

"Many of you may be under the impression that the Dene are happy now simply because some have a few jobs or contracts, and that we are involved in a joint venture with Esso at Norman Wells . . . Let me assure you that we're not at all happy with the way the Norman Wells decision was made.

We are not happy with someone else overrunning our land and taking our resources. We're not happy with the promises made by the government at the time IPL and Esso were given the green light and then twisted beyond recognition later.

When the decision was made, we accepted the inevitable and tried our best to make the project work for us . . . we gave it our best shot, but it's not working. With few exceptions, all the promises of benefits for the Dene resulted in benefits to others."

A Vision of a New Society

Our other main focus has always been political and constitutional change in Denendeh. In 1981, the Dene Nation and the Métis Association drafted a document entitled, Public Govern-

First Conference on the Constitutional Development of the Northwest Territories in January, 1982.
Left to right:
Sam Raddi, president of COPE; Georges Erasmus, president of the Dene Nation; Jim Bourque, president of the Métis Association.

ment for the People of the North, commonly known as the Denendeh Proposal. It is intended to be discussed and changed to suit the requirements of all people who have made the north their home.

In the introduction, Dene Nation president, Georges Erasmus, and Métis president, Jim Bourque wrote:

> "This document is a discussion paper dealing with the issue of achieving an agreement on Aboriginal Rights while working toward political and constitutional change in a way that unites, rather than divides, northern people . . . We believe descendants of the Dene are equal to the task. We believe other northern people are also equal to the task."

The Denendeh proposal is a vision of a new society with a province-like jurisdiction in the western Northwest Territories based on the political style and tradition of the Dene, stressing mutual respect for and co-operation between all northern people — the Dene-Métis majority and other Canadians who share the land. Basic traditions of all cultures will be respected and allowed to develop. It leads to interdependence not assimilation.

Reaction to the proposal has been varied. Some people are outraged and feel threatened by a type of government which they believe would give too much protection to Dene rights. Others see it as a unique opportunity to be part of something exciting, a chance for all people of the north to join together and build a new style of government.

In February 1982, an independent Constitutional Alliance

Nick Sibbeston, of Fort Simpson, was a member of the Legislative Assembly from 1970 to 1974, and was re-elected in 1979.

was formed from members of the Legislative Assembly, the Dene Nation, the Métis Association, COPE, and ITC (Inuit Tapirisat of Canada).

A territorial plebiscite in April indicated that the majority wanted the Northwest Territories divided into two political jurisdictions. In July 1982, the Constitutional Alliance created the Nunavut Constitutional Forum and the Western Constitutional Forum with a mandate to draw up a blueprint for the future of the territories. The Dene Nation and the Métis Association actively participate in the Western Forum.

At the western constitutional conference in September 1982, people of different traditions came closer to an understanding. Chairman Nick Sibbeston expressed his pleasure, "This has been one of the best meetings between natives and non-natives in the last few years. We're finally beginning to act like northerners."

During the first Canadian constitutional conference on aboriginal rights in 1983, our Native leaders sat at the discussion table with the prime minister and premiers of the provinces. When our leaders spoke, they were heard on national television by all of Canada. We will continue to be involved with all Native people to enshrine our rights in the Canadian Constitution. However, our situation is unique in Canada. We are the majority of the resident population in Denendeh. Unlike most Canadian Indians we don't live on reservations and are still able to negotiate with the federal government the ways in which our rights will be recognized and respected. Along with the other people living in Denendeh we are not locked into a provincial or any other system. The Government of the Northwest Territories has declared itself to be a provisional structure, and creative solutions and alternatives are possible.

William Bonnetplume depicts the core of all northern problems.

Stephen Kakfwi, of Fort Good Hope, was elected president of the Dene Nation in September 1983.

Like all nations with ancient roots, our culture has given reason to our world. Even with so many new pressures, our style of government is unchanged, the languages we speak are still our own. Our drums bring us together as in the past. Our songs are still sung for the happiness of a good day, in thanksgiving to the Creator, or in prayerful supplication.

Our struggle for self-determination is not new. Faced with recent challenges we have learned to adapt to situations as well as to influence history in Denendeh. Whenever we face hard times we draw strength from the laws given to us at the beginning of time. We remember the words and significance of Yamoria and other leaders and prophets. They help us to endure with dignity in times of oppression; to be creative in our

Dene leaders at the National Assembly in 1980.

Left to right:
Georges Erasmus, James Wah-shee, Richard Nerysoo, and Paul Andrew.

A Dene leadership meeting in April 1984.

Left to right:
Jim Antoine, chief of Fort Simpson from 1974 to 1976, and from February, 1979; Stanley Sanguez of Jean Marie River; and Gabe Hardisty, chief of Fort Wrigley from January, 1978 to August, 1981, and from June, 1983.

freedom; to protect and enrich our Dene heritage; and to share our knowledge, our wisdom and our vision of the world with those who have come to live in our homeland. Today we still remember the Dene laws and realize more than ever our responsibility to the land, to her resources, and to each other. We believe our responsibility is greater today and must be carried out by us for the future generations. Many people share our vision, appreciate our perspective, and work with us in our struggle for self-determination.

Our Dene Nation is both old and new. Our ancestors did not need a strong centralized organization as they lived their lives without disturbance. Our nation remains the same but circumstances led us to shape new ways of being a nation. In 1969, coming from five languages and five tribes, and from sixteen villages separated by large distances, we united to form the Indian Brotherhood of the Northwest Territories. Since then we have created strong bonds of unity among ourselves; we have learned to listen to each other and to act together. With all the frustrations and hopes of the past fifteen years, the greatest achievement we can be proud to celebrate is the new life which we have fostered in our Dene Nation, the new life which our nation has created in every one of us.

At our leadership meeting in April 1984, Charlie Snowshoe, vice-president of the Dene Nation, expressed what is in all our hearts:

". . . my belief is that if we all stand up together and fight for what we want, and not give up, we might accomplish something for ourselves and for the future of our children."

A feeling that defies description swept over me as I stood there alone and surveyed the wonders of creation. There, stretched out before me from my very feet to the distant blue horizon, were rolling hills, lakes, rivers, valleys, trees, open spaces.

JOHN TETSO

The 10,000 square kilometre delta of the Mackenzie River forms a maze of lakes and channels which continue to provide a rich harvest of muskrats for the Dene, Inuvialuit and Métis.

Drum Lake is in the heart of the Mountain Indians' territory.

Fireweed.

Sunset through a frosted window.

"In the past, I've had some hard times and sad times, and I'm still going that way. It's just life. We didn't do all this just to be rich. We just carry the future for our old grandmothers. I love my grandmother even though I was small back then. I think about her and then I get brave again and I start smilin' and going."

MARY KONDI

Julia Crapeau and Eileen Liske.

In spring, the Dene of Fort Good Hope traditionally hunt in Tuyétah, an area of thousands of lakes inhabited by beavers and muskrats. Along with hard work comes time to enjoy life after the long winter.

"We want a settlement where we can keep our land till the end of the earth and not have our future relatives to have to fight for it again and again, possibly till our land is ours no more. We want to keep our land, we don't want money. . . . We want a settlement where not only us and our children will be happy, but (also) our great-grandchildren. A million times our thoughts will be happy."

AGNES ANDRE

Jatonia Nitsiza of Lac La Martre.

At the winter camp of George and Florence Barnaby, near the Sans Sault Rapid. Two-year old Joseph, one of their six children, is eager to work, whether to help his father stretch marten pelts or to do the laundry.

I HEARD A BIRD SING

I heard a bird singing in the dark of
    December
a magical thing! and sweet to
    remember.
We are nearer to spring
than we were in September.
I heard a bird sing in the dark of
    December.

Overleaf:
*Ernest Liske paints his boat.
Canoes, wooden boats, or flat-
bottom scows are used, depending
on the kind of water one travels,
and whether the craft is used for
fishing, freighting, or travelling.*

*"Our life is part of the land. We live on the land and
are satisfied with what we get from it. No one
person owns the land, it belongs to all of us. We choose
where we want to go and our choice is respected by
others whether in the settlement or in the bush. We
have no word in our language that means
wilderness, as anywhere we go is our home."*

GEORGE BARNABY

*Gabriel and Dorothy Cotchilley and family at their fish camp. Gabriel
was chief of Fort Good Hope until 1971.*

*A trapper's home during winter. The tent is heated by a small woodstove,
and illuminated by a gas lamp.*

Verna Crapeau and son. Baby swings, made of two ropes and a blanket are hung in the mainroom or over the parents' bed.

YOUNG PEOPLE GO HOME AGAIN

We must listen to our Spirit once
 again
And apologize for running away from her
 back then
We must be the one to play the role of
 the animal's friend
Or there will be no tomorrow for the land
 or for them

We must build from what we know once
 again
For our knowledge is the Spirit's as our
 friend
No one else can tell us how to love the
 land again
And we must hurry or it soon will be the
 end.

The adopted family of Michel Louis and Therese Eyakfwo of Rae.

Right:
Bernadette Crapeau of Dettah.

60

"Development has to be something that is transferring control to the people. If you look at either pipelines, or sawmills, or dams, or new mines, we are not against any of those kinds of things. What we are saying is that development should be orderly, it should be planned, it should be at the pace of the local people, it should benefit local people."

GEORGES ERASMUS

"We love the Mackenzie River, that's our life. It shelters us when it storms and it feeds us when there is hunger. It takes care of its children, the native people."

JOACHIM BONNETROUGE

Oil tanks at Norman Wells.

Bella T'seleie of Fort Good Hope.

"It's not as some people keep referring to us as
looking back. We are not looking back. We do not
want to remain static. We do not want to stop the
clock of time. Our old people, when they talk about
how the Dene ways should be kept by young
people, they are not looking back, they are looking
forward. They are looking as far ahead into the
future as they possibly can. So are we all."

GEORGES ERASMUS

Waterfall upstream from Fossil Lake.

We are so deeply spiritual people,
It's not easy to become religious.

Graveyards such as this one in Hay River are always located in beautiful places. Graves are usually fenced or covered.

In July 1983, the Dene of Lac La Martre gather at the grave of Jacques Nade-Beaulieu, or Yezi-Eta, the founder of their community, to celebrate in prayer the 100th anniversary of his death.

Naedzo, of Dogrib descent, was recognized as a prophet, and Dene from surrounding communities came to him for advice. He died in Fort Franklin in 1973, at the age of 83, after being blind for many years.

Snare Lake in mid-winter.

K'áhba is the ptarmigan, ***Mí*** is a fishnet, ***Túé*** is a lake, so ***K'áhbamítúé*** is "the lake where we net ptarmigans" (Colville Lake). Old fish nets are stretched among the willows on the lake shore, and ptarmigans fly into the nets.

Angele Oudzi (opposite) and her son Joseph, of Colville Lake.

WINTER

Winter coming
Blows freezing winds
Before the days
That stand still

All life retreats
To cradles
Hung
In shaded trees

Steam from coffee cup
Blurs waves
    of brittle cold
Lapping against
    frosted window
    and sill

Overleaf:
Helen and Michel Drybone.

Jesse Hardisty of Fort Wrigley.

"I am always made very proud when I listen to our old People. They have so much knowledge of all the things that have gone before. They view the present through with wise old eyes that gives the younger people far more strength to continue. They have more understanding of what is happening now than anyone else gives them credit for."

JAMES WAH-SHEE

Marie Tobie and granddaughter Tina Sangris.

Winter winds shape the snow into artistic forms.

"We like to be free; travelling where we want and when we want. We were this way in the old days . . ."

PHILIP SIMBA

In a country with so few roads, winter is the best time for travel, as the rivers and lakes are frozen and the land is covered with snow. Winter lasts so long, that some Dene languages have the same word for "winter" and "year".

Burned forest between Rae and Fort Providence.

"As a Dene I have a certain way of looking at the world around me. I am a well-educated person. The forests have been the school I went to. Nature has been the book I read. The animals have been my teachers. The seasons became my calendar. My needs are the clock I work by; my senses and my imagination, the tools of my survival."

Snow sculptured by the wind.

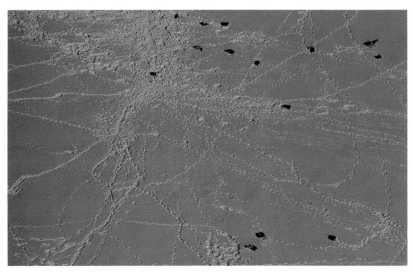

Caribou tracks, as seen from the air. Caribou migrate northward to the "barren lands" in spring, and back to the forested country in fall.

Overleaf:
Great Bear Lake in June. Some summers, drifting ice lasts as late as July 20th.

DENE

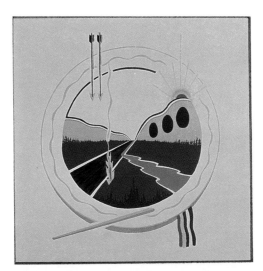

DENENDEH

 **UNIVERSITY OF ALBERTA**
LIBRARIES

VICTORIA ISLAND

2295

Bay

P9-EDZ-641

Fr. Jean Allégret
+omi

Arctic Circle

Coppermine

Bathurst Inlet

Coppermine River

Back River

Sahtú
(Great Bear Lake)

Gamètì
(Rae Lake)

Wekwètì
(Snare Lake)

Tsòtì
(Lac La Martre)

Bèhchokò
(Rae)

Sòmbak'è
(Yellowknife)

ʔedzo
(Edzo)

Tᶲehda
(Dettah)

Łútsëlk'e
(Snowdrift)

Łíidlį Kóę́
(Fort Simpson)

Tthedzéhk'édéli Kóę́
(Jean Marie River)

River)

Zhahti kóę́
(Fort Providence)

Tucho
(Great Slave Lake)

Denínu
(Fort Resolution)

K'áágee Tú
(Kakisa Lake)

Kátł'o Dehé
(Hay River)

Tsąmba K'é
(Pine Point)

Tthebachaghé
(Fort Smith)

SASK.

Sambaa K'ee
(Trout Lake)

ALTA.

Tthebatthié
(Fort Fitzgerald)

Hay River)

Desnedé
(Slave R.)

Lake Athabasca

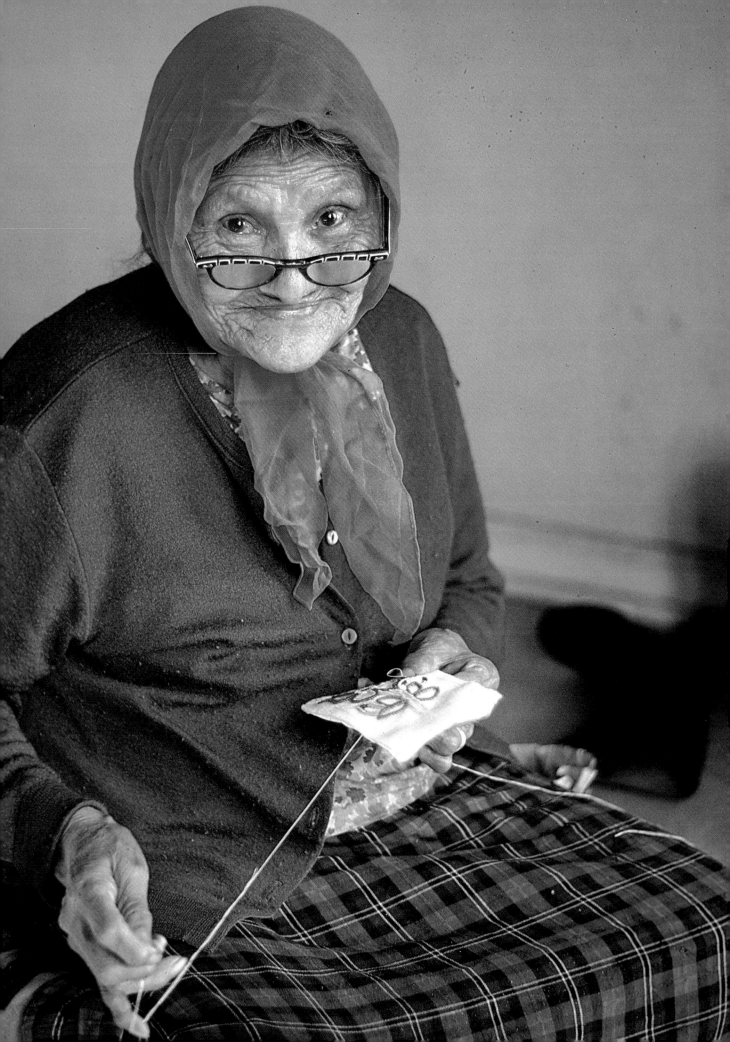

The church at Rae-Edzo, the largest Dene community. Women sit on one side, men on the other.

Jimmy and Seraphine Betsina.
"Life is to be lived every moment to the full"

Shortly before her death at the age
of 86, Marie Charlo beads a vamp
or "upper" for a moccasin.

Patricia Modeste of Fort Franklin.

Right:
Maggy was a Hareskin, renowned for her hunting and trapping skills and her artistic beadwork. Her husband Barney Fisher came from the south in the early 1900's and settled in Fort Good Hope. "He never learned a Dene language, their friends recall, and she spoke her own kind of English, so they must have found a way to communicate somehow". Maggy died in 1979 at the age of ninety-five.

Northern lights, Aurora Borealis.

Salt Plains near Fort Smith. These are flat, mostly open areas with many salt springs which provided salt for the people and the buffalo.

"Our real parents have long deceased, and this land is like our own father and mother."

BRUNO APPLE

Paul Wright and grandson David at Drum Lake. Paul was Band Councillor in Fort Norman in 1964 and 1976, and chief from September 1977 to July 1984.

Jonas Crapeau, on Great Slave Lake.

Mary Dene spent a great part of the summer making dry fish. The fish were cleaned, gutted, hung over poles in the sun for two or three days, then smoked over a smouldering fire in a "smoke tent". Dry fish was used in winter as food for people and dogs.

"This land is sort of our industry, providing us with shelter, food, income, similar to the industries down south supporting the White peoples."

CHARLIE CHOCOLATE

Roger Boniface (left), Martha Rabiska tanning a moose hide, and Stanley Cook, of Fort Good Hope.

*Fishing on the Mountain River in
October just before freeze-up.*

*Mary Rose Crapeau hanging
whitefish to dry.*

Cleaning lake trout in Fort Franklin.

"The land, and all it provides for our people has been the very spirit of the Dene way of life. From the land came our religion . . . from the land came our life . . . from the land came our powerful medicine . . . from the land came our way of life."

GEORGE BLONDIN

A Dene on Great Bear Lake pulls his fishnet from under five feet of ice. Handling wet nets and fish is one of the coldest tasks of winter.

Marten pelts. The Dene also trap weasel, red, blue, silver, cross, and white fox, lynx, muskrat, mink, beaver, and otter.

"I am strictly a trapper. I was born and raised in the bush. When I was seven years old, that is when I first started learning about bush life. I used to watch my brothers come back from the trap line. They would bring back marten and when they would go hunting, they would always bring back a moose or caribou. They are good hunters and trappers. They seldom failed when hunting, and I used to envy them because they were good in the bush life. Ever since that time I had one thing in my mind: I wanted to be a trapper. From then on, I tried hard to learn the ways of bush life. I learned most everything from my mother. She is a tough woman when it comes to bush life. Through hardships and good times, we always stuck it out. We seldom complained for complaining is not the way of a true trapper. My Mum, she did a good job. She made a good trapper out of me. She taught me to follow in the footsteps of my ancestors. Today I stand out among trappers and I am proud of it."

JEAN MARIE RABISKA

Wilbert Kochon, of Colville Lake, and wolf pelts.

Alice Cli, of Fort Wrigley,
slicing moose meat to be dried.

Some people think they can own the land.
We know that the land owns us.

Paul Wright, Gabriel Etchinele and Ron Erasmus enjoy a tea break
during a meeting at Drum Lake. Above them moose meat dries in the sun.

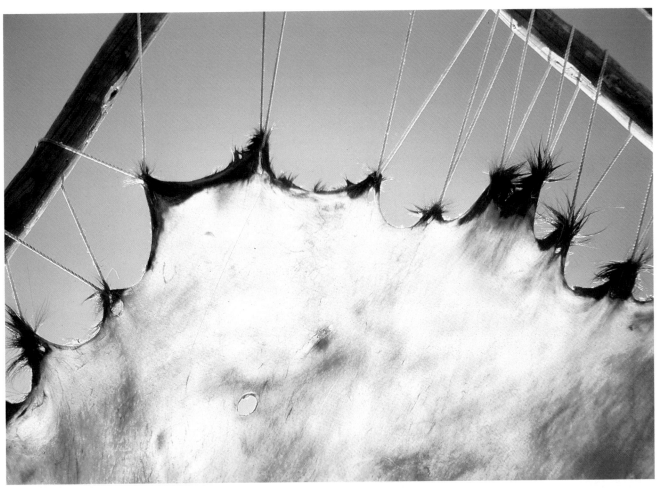

Moose hide stretched on a frame. The inner side has been defleshed, and the hair has been scraped away.

Traditionally Tanned Hides

One of the most basic raw materials of the Dene is the traditionally tanned moose and caribou hide. It is a unique material which cannot be reproduced by industrial tanning techniques. It is strong, light weight, form fast, easy to sew, warm and of characteristic snow white when bleached, or rusty brown when smoke treated for longevity. The smokey aroma is reminiscent of a campfire and is appreciated by all who know it. Its rich golden-brown texture compliments bright beadwork on slippers, mukluks, mitts and jackets.

Tanning moose hide in the traditional way requires much skill and patience.

First the hide is fleshed, scraped of hair, washed and stretched out to dry. Later the hide is scraped again, soaked and scraped again before being wrung out and dried. The next step in the tanning process is the arduous task of working the hide to a supple softness with a large bone scraper. Only then is the hide ready to be browned over a smokey fire.

Caribou hides being bleached in the spring sun, in Snowdrift.

Wood Buffalo National Park, which covers 44,800 square kilometres and straddles the Northwest Territories-Alberta border is home to about 6,000 buffalo. The park is not fenced, and buffalo wandering off the park limits may be hunted.

Dressing a buffalo.

Moose hide stretched on a frame, with the hair partly removed.

Beaver pelts. Beaver are easily shot in spring, but pelts from beaver trapped in winter are of better quality, because the hair is undamaged by the sun.

Benoit Erutse, Norbert Caesar, and Angus Shae at their hunting camp
in May. Portaging canoes from lake to lake is hard work, but there are
relaxing moments in the continuous daylight.

All these Sir Alexander MacKenzie and all these guys
they were sitting in the boat and reading eh
and the poor guys were paddling them around and
they get credit for it and
nobody else:

Mr. So and So discovered the Mackenzie

All that kind of thing but
the poor guy who's at work
you don't hear about

Ted Trindell

Sunset on the Peel River at Fort McPherson.

Left:
Andre Andre of Fort Franklin. To make a snowshoe, a frame made of spruce or birch is bent into shape and held by cross pieces. Then it is laced with "babiche", strips of raw caribou or moose hide.

Right:
Jean Tinqui of Rae builds a canoe. The frame and ribs are cut and shaped with axe and knife, then covered with canvas instead of birch bark, spruce bark or untanned hides, as was done in the past.

A Dene father and son shape a new canvas over a canoe. They will tack it along the gunwale and paint it.

Celine Gargan of Jean Marie River decorates with porcupine quills, the most traditional ornament. The quills are dyed different colors with natural or chemical pigments.

Julienne Taureau makes moccasins from moose hide.

Moose hair and caribou hair tufting

In 1789, Alexander Mackenzie recorded that the local natives' clothing was "decorated with an embroidery of very neat workmanship with porcupine quills and hair of the moose, coloured red, black, yellow, and white."

The moose hair most suitable for tufting is the winter fur, obtained between December and March. It is usually six to eight inches in length and comes from the centre back of the animal. Caribou hair is softer and does not shed as easily. The hair is picked from the hide by hand, sorted by length, washed in soap and water, and dyed. Natural dyes such as berries, bark and leaves are still used but commercial powdered dyes and crepe paper are popular as well.

After dyeing, the hair is dried and ready for sewing. The design is drawn directly on the hide for moccasins and mitts, or on canvas-backed velvet for wall pieces. These outlines are drawn freehand, and not two designs are identical. For the sewing, about 15-20 hairs are held on the pattern, a stitch is made around the hair about ¼" from the end, pulled tight and knotted at the back of the material. This makes the moose hair stand up in a brisk tuft. The long part of the hair is cut off about ¼" from the stitch. The remainder of the hair is used in the same fashion until the outline is filled in. The hair is then sculptured with scissors, resulting in the finished product as we know it.

Right:
Caribou hair tufting by Lucy Sanguez.

Loons painted on a drum by Archie Beaulieu of Rae.

Artifacts from Jean Marie River.

Mass and drum dance (opposite) during the Dene National Assembly at Fort Simpson in Spring 1982. In a church or a meeting place, for a prayer or for a dance, beating reverently as the heartbeat of a person or with all the strength of the Nation, the drum has a deep spiritual meaning, proclaiming freedom for everyone as well as building the community spirit.

Menton Mantla of Lac La Martre plays the drum during a hand game.

DRUMS OF MY FATHER

Many thousands years have passed and yet
The pride and joy of the drums has stayed
In the hearts of the old and the young.

The beat is heard throughout the town
The excitement stirs amongst the people
The children are restless
The women are tireless
And the men are fearless.

The cries of the drum are heard
The people are quiet and listen in calmness
The beat becomes louder, louder and louder
Then quietness.

The beat is heard
The shouts, laughter and song from the drum is
heard
The people are smiling and dancing with dignity
For the pride of the drums shall always remain
with them.

CELINE MACKENZIE

Overleaf:
Handicrafts from Jean Marie River.

The Hand Game

Two teams of an indefinite but equal number of men line up facing each other. Throughout the game the players maintain a kneeling-seated posture. One team at a time operates as the active playing team. Each of its member hides a token in one of his fists. A single member of the other team guesses, by means of a hand signal, and simultaneously for all the players, which fist of each man holds the token.

The style and impact of a hand game in action eludes precise description. The tempo of play is fast and hard, with the deafening clamor of drums and the shouted chant of the drummers accompanying the play. The intensity of the syncopated beat that goes from loud to louder as climaxes in the game occur imparts a driving quality to the play. In response to the throb of the drums, the players of the hiding team move in rhythm. From their hips up, the kneeling men bob, weave, and sway. One part of the play involves a crouching position to reshuffle the concealed token and then the raising of the torso and the offering of the arms folded or outstretched to the guess of the opposing captain. The captain's guess may be delayed for many seconds or even for a few minutes as he calculates the disposition of tokens against him.

After the guess, the rhythmic movements continue as the members of the playing team open their fists to reveal the tokens and after a few seconds again go into the reshuffling crouch.

The two-syllable unit of chanting cry made by the drummers is delivered with wide-open mouth, head thrown back, with strained features by some and at full voice by all.

The members of the opposing team sit quietly watching the action. The guesser for their team is also in bodily repose, although his visual attention to the actions of the playing team is pronounced.

National Museum of Canada, Bulletin 205
The Dogrib Hand Game
by June Helm and Nancy Oestreich Lurie

Kakisa, to the south of Great Slave Lake is a community of about sixty Slavey Dene, established in the early 1960's.

Charles Sayine. A sawmill helps to provide employment and pride to the Dene of Fort Resolution.

Poplar trees at Kakisa.

Trees are born
Trees die
The forest lives.

The most common trees in
Denendeh are white and black
spruce. Other species include
aspen, balsam, poplar, white birch,
tamarack, jack pine, and willow.

"We who live on the land have seen much of the land
   destroyed by fire. In the past we didn't see many
   fires, they are something that have increased only
 * recently. When we see the land burn, we see our
   traditional way of life destroyed, not just a loss in
   dollar value."

JOE MIGWI

Summer games in Rae-Edzo. Traditionally, summer is for visiting, for enjoyment, for strengthening the community spirit, and renewing ties with relatives and friends.

Left to right:
Dino Elleze, Clifford Bonnetrouge, and Scotty Minoza of Fort Providence.

*"I need and love the land I was born and raised on.
Many people find meaning in different things in life.
Native people find meaning in the land and they
need it and they love it . . . Sometimes you stand on
the shore of the lake, you see high waves rolling
onto shore, and it's pushed by winds you can't see.
Soon it's all calm again. In the winter you see
flowers, trees, rivers and streams covered with snow
and frozen. In the spring it all comes back to life.
This has a strong meaning for my people and me
and we need it."*

RAY SONFRERE

*Lac La Martre is home to about 275 Dene, most of whom speak only
their Dogrib language.*

Darlene Barnaby of Fort Good Hope.

Arnold Gargan of Jean Marie River.

Fort Norman at the confluence of the Bear and Mackenzie Rivers.

Fort McPherson, on the Peel River.

The bright colours of the houses have given the name Rainbow Valley
to this district at the north end of Yellowknife, home to about 200 Dene.

"People here are still trying hard to remain
independent. To maintain their own culture and their
own way. There's so much pressure on the people
these days and everything has to be done right
away. Pipelines, highways, gas lands and dams.
There comes a point when people get snowed
under. If we just had enough time on our own, we
could work it out together . . . at our own speed."

ROBERT CLEMENT

"The old saying is a good saying that goes — Just because an Indian is quiet doesn't mean he doesn't know anything."

JAMES WAH-SHEE

Fireweed.

Michael Beaulieu of Fort Resolution is a descendant of François Beaulieu, one of the guides who took Alexander Mackenzie down the Mackenzie River to the Arctic Ocean in 1789 and to the Pacific Ocean in 1793.

At freeze-up time, the thin ice over a river is sometimes broken by the
current, the wind, or heavier ice, and left standing through the winter.

Previous page:
The Slave River below Mountain
Rapids, near Fort Smith. In the
early 1980s, a controversy arose
over a proposed dam near this site.

*At the Arctic Circle, the sun does not set on June 21. The further
north, the more "nights" the sun is continuously visible, and the
higher it remains in the sky. Fifteen exposures on the same slide frame
show the positions of the sun every ten minutes from 11 p.m. to 1:30 a.m.*

Alfred Baillargeon hauls small logs to Dettah. Snowmobiles have replaced many dogteams, but they are expensive, fragile, and difficult to maintain.

Dettah in springtime.

To get water in winter, holes are cut through the ice, or ice blocks are hauled home and melted. In most communities now, water is delivered regularly by water truck.

The community of Arctic Red River, at the confluence of the Mackenzie and Arctic Red Rivers, has a present population of about 135.

The Dene Logo and The Legend of Yamoria

Many years ago, before the whiteman came into this country, the Creator sent a special man, Yamoria, who travelled into our land. He put everything into its rightful place and got rid of whatever was harmful to people. By doing this, he set laws for people and animals to follow. Until this very day, we are still holding onto them.

There were large beavers living in Sahtú (Great Bear Lake). People who lived in this area would travel across the lake by canoe to hunt the caribou. The beavers did not like them to travel across the lake so they would get as close as possible to the canoes and splash their tails hoping to tip them over. When Yamoria heard about that, he went to Sahtú and told the people that he would chase the beavers away.

Yamoria started chasing the beavers around the lake. The big beavers immediately went down Sahtú Dé (Bear River) but the younger ones were harder to chase towards the river. During the time that Yamoria was chasing the younger ones around the lake, the bigger beavers had built a dam on the river and that's

where the Sahtú Dé Rapids are to this very day. Yamoria got the younger ones to head down Sahtú Dé and then chased them all down the river to where Tulit'a (Fort Norman) is now situated.

At the confluence of the two rivers, Sahtú Dé (Bear) and Dehcho (Mackenzie), he killed two medium beavers and one small one. The larger ones still living continued down our Great River Dehcho. After killing the three beavers, he stretched and pegged the three hides on the south face of Kwetenị?aá (Bear Rock Mountain). You can see the impression they made to this day.

From the top of Kwetenị?aá, he shot two arrows at the confluence of the two rivers and he said, "as long as this earth shall last you shall call them Yamoria's arrows." Still to this day you can see two big poles sticking out of the River. Even after each spring, when the ice goes, there are always two big poles sticking out of the river.

After shooting the two arrows into the river he brought the beavers that he killed up the Dehcho River about twenty-five kilometres from the confluence. There he slept and where he had cooked the beavers, the grease that had drizzled from them started to burn and until this day that fire continues to burn.

The symbol of the three beavers pelts on Kwetenị?aá (Bear Rock Mountain) and the forever-burning fire up river from that mountain are signs on the land as a reminder of the teachings of the legends. If we remember and live them, if we take the signs set on the land for us as our symbols, we will survive as a nation.

The five-colour ribbons are for the five tribes of the Dene Nation. The logo was first painted on a traditional Dene drum.

Chronology

1967

January
Yellowknife is declared capital of the Northwest Territories. In March Stuart Hodgson is appointed Commissioner, and John Parker Deputy Commissioner.

March
Thebacha Association is organized in Fort Smith.

A branch of the Indian-Eskimo Association is established in the Northwest Territories.

July/August
Communities in the Mackenzie Valley are brought together to celebrate Canada's centennial year. The Dene use the time for sharing common problems and common hopes.

Some members of the Company of Young Canadians come from southern Canada to the Great Slave Lake region.

October
The Dene organize community leadership workshops in the lower Mackenzie region.

Volume II of "A Survey of the Contemporary Indians of Canada" is released. This study was commissioned by the Department of Citizenship & Immigration in 1964 and was directed by H. B. Hawthorn. The report rejects "termination" of Indian status and Indian rights as a policy option.

1968

January
The First Dene Member of the Territorial Council is appointed — former Chief John Charlie Tetlichi of Fort McPherson.

June
Bud Orange is re-elected Member of Parliament for the Northwest Territories.

Leon Sambele and Steve Iveson from Denendeh meet with the Manitoba Indian Brotherhood.

July
Canadian Indians form the National Indian Brotherhood to unite their provincial organizations. Walter Deiter is the first president.

Pierre E. Trudeau replaces Lester B. Pearson as Prime Minister. Jean Chretien replaces Arthur Laing as Minister of Indian Affairs and Northern Development.

"Indian Act Consultation" meeting in Yellowknife.

Chief Jimmy Bruneau leads the boycott of the annual Treaty ceremony at Fort Rae.

October
Commercial fishing is organized in Lac La Martre.

The Yukon Native Brotherhood is formed in Whitehorse. Elijah Smith is elected president.

December
The Canadian government sets up a task force on "Northern Oil Development." Its chief purpose is the formation of a Mackenzie Valley pipeline corridor.

Major discoveries of oil and gas at Prudhoe Bay, Alaska.

The Company of Young Canadians, both southerners and northerners, begins research into Treaties 8 and 11.

Anthropologists June Helm, Beryl Gillespie and David M. Smith undertake studies and recordings in various Dene communities. Their studies will last a number of years.

The Deninoo Association is formed in Fort Resolution by both Métis and Dene.

The Adult Vocational Training Centre (AVTC) located at Fort Smith begins training heavy equipment operators.

1969

January/February
George Manuel and Father Maurice Goutier, OMI, hold community leadership meetings.

February
Morris Lafferty and Adeline Hardisty of Fort Simpson, Mona Jacob and Frank Laviolette of Fort Smith, Gabriel Gargan and Ted Landry of Fort Providence, Paul Baton and Jonas Neyelle of Fort Norman, Jim Lafferty and Alexander King of Fort Resolution, Philip Blake of Fort McPherson, and Jonas Jerome of Inuvik agree to serve on a committee set up to establish the Native Brotherhood.

At the Territorial Council session, Chief Jimmy Bruneau of Fort Rae opposes the move of Fort Rae people to the planned townsite of Edzo.

May
Harold Cardinal visits Fort Smith.

June
The Committee for Original People's Entitlement (COPE) is formed by the Native people of the western Arctic, headquartered in Inuvik, and with Agnes Semmler serving as president.

Jean Chretien, minister of Indian Affairs, releases the "White Paper". It proposes to transfer the responsibility and obligations of the Crown towards Indians to the provincial and territorial administrations. Indians across Canada are enraged.

July
Sunrise Association is formed in Hay River, by Ernie Sibbeston, Virginie Fabian, Alphonse Cardinal, Frank Norn, Daniel Sonfrere, Ted Bugghins, Nora Villebrun, Gladys Bugghins, Antoinette Norn, Ed Fabian, George Sibbeston. The president is Raymond Paul.

The Chiefs refuse to attend any more "Advisory Council Meetings" arranged by the Federal Government. The Dene agree that an Indian Brotherhood should be formed in the north.

August
Pierre Trudeau, speaks in Vancouver: "By aboriginal rights, this really means saying: 'We were here before you. You came and took the land away from us, and perhaps you cheated us by giving us some worthless things in return for vast expanses of land, and we want to reopen this question. We want you to preserve our aboriginal rights and to restore them to us.' And our answer is . . . NO."

September
First teachers' education program for northern Native people, the "Experimental Teacher Education Program" begins in Yellowknife. It became part of AVTC in 1970.

October
The Dene and their sixteen chiefs form the Indian Brotherhood of the Northwest Territories.

Jean Chretien, minister of Indian Affairs, declares in Yellowknife: "Seventy-five percent of government jobs will be filled by northern residents by 1977".

November
Judge Morrow, of the Northwest Territories Territorial Court, dismisses the conviction of Joe Drybone, a Dene accused of being drunk "off the reserve", according to the Indian Act. Morrow pronounces that the federal Indian Act violates Joe Drybone's rights under the Bill of Rights to "equality before the law".

December
Prime Minister Trudeau appoints Lloyd Barber Indian Claims Commissioner.

1970

January
Natural gas is discovered at Atkinson Point, near Tuktoyaktuk.

February
Following a meeting of the sixteen chiefs in Yellowknife, the Indian Brotherhood of the Northwest Territories (IBNWT) is incorporated. Roy Daniels is elected interim president. On staff are Barney Masuzumi, James Wah-Shee, Francis Blackduck, and Mike Canadian.

May
The government task force on "Northern Oil Development" declares that a Mackenzie Valley pipeline for oil or gas would be in the "national interest".

June
The Tree of Peace Friendship Centre is established in Yellowknife.

The Indian Chiefs of Alberta present "Citizens Plus" to Prime Minister Trudeau. It is their answer to Jean Chretien's 1969 "White Paper".

George Manuel is elected president of the National Indian Brotherhood. (Re-elected in 1972, he will step down in September, 1976.)

July
First Annual Conference of Arctic Native People in Coppermine.

Queen Elizabeth II visits Yellowknife.

August
The first annual General Assembly of the Indian Brotherhood is held in the United Church basement in Yellowknife.

The federal government issues "Northern Pipeline Guidelines", a general framework designed to help industry prepare their pipeline applications.

First Northern Games for Native people of the Northwest Territories, Yukon, and Alaska.

Trout Lake Dene build the Trout Lake Fishing Lodge.

December
James Rabesca is elected to Territorial Council. James Wah-Shee unsuccessfully ran in Yellowknife.

"Trapping is my Life", written by John Tetso, a Slavey living near Fort Simpson, is published by Peter Martin Associates. He is the first Dene to have a book published.

1971

January
The Indian Brotherhood establishes a Native language broadcasting unit. Its radio programs are broadcast over Yellowknife station CFYK by Antoine Mountain. Soon, the Inuvik station broadcasts Loucheux and Inuktitut, in co-operation with COPE.

James Wah-Shee is elected inerim president of the Indian Brotherhood. He travels up and down the Mackenzie Valley on consultation tours with community people.

March
For the first time, the Department of the Secretary of State provides core funding for the operation of the Indian Brotherhood.

James Wah-Shee is reaffirmed as president of the Indian Brotherhood for a two-year term.

April
The Newspaper "The Indian Brotherhood Report" is first printed and distributed to all Native homes in the Mackenzie Valley. It becomes "Native Press" in May.

Gerald Sutton, lawyer, is hired by the Indian Brotherhood to assist with treaty research.

July
The General Assembly of the Indian Brotherhood at Fort Rae objects to the implementation of the "White Paper" policy and reaffirms its determination to have the land and treaty question settled before any more land development takes place.

August
Chief Pierre Catholique of Snowdrift confronts National Parks representatives about their plan to make a park out of his peoples' hunting ground.

Chief Ed Bird of Fort Smith, secretary-treasurer of the Indian Brotherhood dies in Yellowknife.

October
George Manuel (now President of the National Indian Brotherhood) visits Yellowknife, Dettah and Rae-Edzo.

Inuit Tapirisat, COPE, and the Indian Brotherhood meet in Edmonton and form an alliance.

The Yukon Association of Non-Status Indians (YANSI) is formed.

December
The U.S. Congress passes the Alaska Native Claims Settlement Act.

1972

January
Joe Tobie begins broadcasting in Dogrib on CBC Radio.

The Chief Jimmy Bruneau School officially opens in Rae-Edzo.

February
Indian Brotherhood Leadership Meeting in Fort Franklin. George Manuel, president of the National Indian Brotherhood, is a guest.

March
Founding conference of the Native Council of Canada in Ottawa. Sixteen Métis from the western Arctic attend and also plan to form a Métis organization in the Northwest Territories. A steering committee is set up with Dave McNabb, president; Charles Overvold, vice-president; and Carol Berens, secretary-treasurer. In April, the Métis Association of the Northwest Territories establishes its headquarters in Hay River.

April
The Department of Indian Affairs re-opens its office in Yellowknife.

Prime Minister Trudeau announces that an all-weather highway along the full length of the Mackenzie Valley will be built.

The Métis Association of the Northwest Territories establishes its "Winter Warmth" program to repair Native peoples' houses.

May
The National Indian Brotherhood meets in Yellowknife.

The Indian Brotherhood hires four field workers to conduct a health study in Denendeh.

June
The Department of Indian Affairs announces its version of a treaty settlement: Indian reserves for the Dene, or cash in return for the extinguishment of all rights.

July
The two pipeline proponents, "Northwest Project Study Group" and "Gas Arctic Systems Study Group" join to form "Canadian Arctic Gas Study Limited".

August
The Indian Brotherhood Annual General Assembly is held in Fort McPherson. James Wah-Shee is re-elected president and John Itsi, vice-president. The president of the Métis Association, Dave McNabb and representatives of the Yukon Native Brotherhood and of the National Indian Brotherhood attend the assembly. Fort McPherson people enjoy drum dancing again, as they had not had such dances for a long time.

The presidents of seven Canadian and Alaskan Native organizations form the "Federation of Natives North of Sixty".

Sam Raddi is elected president of COPE; re-elected every two years to March 1982.

"Hire North" project starts to provide employment for 250 people of the Northwest Territories for two years, to hand-clear the 1,100 kilometre route of the Mackenzie Highway from Fort Simpson to Tuktoyaktuk.

October
Wally Firth, a Métis from Fort McPherson, is elected as NDP member from the Northwest Territories to the House of Commons.

1973

January
The first annual General Assembly of the Métis and Non-Status Native Association of the Northwest Territories is held in Hay River. Dave McNabb is elected president.

The Supreme Court of Canada is split 3-3 on the validity of aboriginal rights of the Nishga Indians: this landmark decision is an immense moral victory for the Nishga and all other Native people. One week later, Trudeau confesses "Perhaps you have more legal rights than we thought you had when we did the White Paper."

Chief Daniel Sonfrere of Hay River requests reservation status for his village. He feared that expansion of the townsite would one day overrun Dene land.

February
In the case of Jeanette Lavell, the Supreme Court of Canada maintains that an Indian woman marrying a non-Indian man loses her Indian status.

March
At Wounded Knee, South Dakota, Indians briefly hold eleven people hostage in memory of the massacre of 300 Indians there in 1890.

Old Naedzo, the Dene Prophet, dies.

April
The Dene present a "Caveat" covering their traditional lands.

Aklavik, Fort Resolution, Fort Smith, Hay River and Yellowknife are linked to the CBC Television Network.

The House of Commons Standing Committee on Indian Affairs endorses the National Indian Brotherhood's demands for recognition of aboriginal rights.

June
Judge Morrow of the Supreme Court of the NWT spends the summer listening to the Dene speak about Treaties 8 and 11. He holds caveat hearings in the communities. On September 6, he rules in favor of the Dene and upholds their claim to 1,000,000 square kilometres of land.

The Métis Association of the Northwest Territories in a telegram to Minister Jean Chretien, proclaims its support for the Treaty Indians' version of the treaties.

Due to financial difficulties, most of the staff of the Métis Association, including the executive, are either fired or resign. An interim finance Committee administers the association until the summer of 1974.

Indian Affairs offices in Ottawa are occupied by Indian Youth.

July
Indian Brotherhood Annual General Assembly in Yellowknife.

Fort Rae Drummers perform at the Mariposa Folk Festival in Toronto. This is the first time Dene musicians are recognized in the south.

August
A declaration on aboriginal rights by the Federal government proposes to negotiate the form of compensation to Native groups in exchange for the extinguishment of their traditional interest in the land.

October
The Indian Brotherhood installs radio telephones in all communities of the Mackenzie Valley.

November
The Council for Yukon Indians (CYI) is formed by a union of the Yukon Association of Non-Status Indians and the Yukon Native Brotherhood.

Bill Wacko's report on alcohol abuse is presented to Territorial Council.

December
The Indian Brotherhood hires eight researchers to document how the Dene have used their land in the past.

1974

January
Fort Wrigley people tell Jean Chretien that they do not want the Mackenzie Highway to be built near their community.

February
The Indian Brotherhood hires eighteen field workers to work in the Dene communities.

The Hay River Indian Reserve is established.

March
The Mackenzie Valley Pipeline Inquiry is established by Order-in-Council, with Mr. Justice T. R. Berger as Commissioner. Preliminary hearings are held in April, May and September in Yellowknife, Inuvik, Whitehorse and Ottawa.

The Northern Canada Power Commission plans to build dams on the Bear River to supply electricity for the proposed Mackenzie Valley pipeline. Chief George Kodakin of Fort Franklin travels to Ottawa to express his people's opposition to the damming of the Bear River.

The Métis board of directors and the Dene chiefs meet in Fort Franklin and agree to participate in the Berger Inquiry.

Fort Smith Museum officially opens.

June
Dogrib chiefs and band councillors request Commissioner Hodgson to prohibit the sale of liquor to Dogrib people. They are refused.

The first joint General Assembly of the Métis and Treaty Indians is held in Fort Good Hope. They plan to work toward joining the two organizations.

July
Wally Firth is re-elected NDP Member of Parliament for the Northwest Territories.

The Snowdrift Co-op buys out the local store.

Jim Antoine, twenty-five, is elected Chief of Fort Simpson. He is the youngest chief in Denendeh.

DIAND opens the Office of Native Claims in Ottawa.

August
The Native Communications Society (NCS) is incorporated and takes over the publication of "Native Press".

Judd Buchanan is appointed Minister of Indian Affairs and Northern Development to replace Jean Chretien.

Métis Association holds its second Annual General Meeting in Fort Smith. Rick Hardy is elected president and Charles Overvold, vice-president.

Roaring Rapids Community Hall officially opens in Fort Smith.

September
The annual General Assembly of the Indian Brotherhood is held in Fort Wrigley. James Wah-Shee is re-elected president, John Tutcho of Fort Franklin, vice-president. Five regional vice-presidents are also elected: Henry Beaver, Alexis Arrowmaker, Jim Antoine, Paul Andrew and Tadit Francis.

October
Dr. Lloyd Barber, Indian Claims Commissioner for Canada, speaks on aboriginal rights in Yellowknife.

November
Sixty-one percent of the Fort Resolution people vote in favour of rationing alcohol. Prohibition is also proposed in Fort Rae and Fort Franklin.

Aklavik votes against the establishment of a liquor store in their community.

December
All through Denendeh, field workers discuss unity between the Indian Brotherhood and the Métis Association. Indian and Métis leaders meet to discuss the merger.

The RCMP holds a two-week in-service training course for its senior constables, entitled "Native Extremism".

The Indian Brotherhood organizes five regional workshops on alcohol.

"The Fourth World: An Indian Reality," by George Manuel and Michael Posluns is published by Collier Macmillan.

The Northern Careers Program begins to train Native people on the job for positions of greater responsibility in the Federal Government.

1975

January
Indian Affairs Minister Judd Buchanan states that if land claims negotiations were going to drag on over the next few years, he would not hold back the Mackenzie Valley Pipeline.

Chief Jimmy Bruneau, respected Dogrib leader and chief for over fifty years, dies in Rae.

March
Judge Thomas Berger begins the formal Mackenzie Valley Pipeline hearings in Yellowknife.

James Wah-Shee of Fort Rae, president of the Indian Brotherhood, and George Barnaby of Fort Good Hope are elected to serve on Territorial Council. For the first time, this council is a fully-elected body, except for the Commissioner who is still appointed by Ottawa.

COPE, the Métis Association, and the Indian Brotherhood speak with one voice: "No pipeline until land claims are settled."

In Fort Simpson, the Ko Go Choe Society starts to control Lapointe Hall and plans to begin programs in child care, adult education, alcohol rehabilitation, senior citizens housing, education, research, and youth concerns.

April
The Indian Brotherhood and the Métis Association choose fourteen representatives to negotiate their joint land claims and hold their first meeting with Judd Buchanan. The talks come to a standstill, due to differing views of the Brotherhood and the Métis.

The Berger Inquiry holds the first of the community hearings in Aklavik.

May
The Native Courtworkers Association is formed to begin community work, assist people in conflict with the law, and train Dene in criminal and civil matters. Gail Cyr, who was instrumental in forming the association, is the first employee.

June
James Wah-Shee addresses the General Synod of the Anglican Church of Canada. The Synod passes a resolution in support of the Indian people's struggle.

Foothills Pipe Lines of Calgary submits the first part of an application to build an all-Canadian 1300 kilometres Mackenzie Valley natural gas pipeline.

July
The Dene refuse to negotiate through the Office of Native Claims, set up by the federal government.

James Wah-Shee, Territorial Councillor, tables a motion in Council asking for a ten-year residency before people in the Northwest Territories could vote. The motion is defeated.

At the second joint General Assembly of the Indian Brotherhood and Métis Association in Fort Simpson, delegates unanimously adopt the Dene Declaration.

Nick Sibbeston, a Métis of Fort Simpson, graduates as the first Native lawyer in the NWT.

At its national convention, the New Democractic Party supports a just land claims settlement for the Native people of the north, and the right of the Northwest Territories to self-government.

August
The First conference for Native women (Métis, Inuit and Dene) is held in Pangnirtung.

Third annual Métis General Assembly in Fort Norman followed by the first Native Talent Show.

September
The Canadian Conference of Catholic Bishops issues "Northern Development — At What Cost?", a strong statement in support of the northern Native People, and of a more responsible stewardship of northern resources.

Project North, a coalition of the five major Christian churches in Canada, is formed to support the struggle of northern Canadian Native peoples.

The book, "As Long As This Land Shall Last", by René Fumoleau is published by McClelland and Stewart.

Oxfam-Canada announces its support of the Dene position.

Indian Brotherhood opens a southern support office in Ottawa.

The World Council of Indigenous People (WCIP) is established with George Manuel as president.

Christine Horesay is the first Dene school principal in the Northwest Territories, on the Hay River reserve.

October
The National Energy Board begins its hearings into the Mackenzie Valley natural gas pipeline.

November
Cree and Inuit in northern Quebec sign the James Bay Agreement. They give up their rights to one million square kilometres of ancestral territory, in return for $225 million in cash compensation over the next twenty years, a limited level of local self-government and some rights over two specific categories of lands.

December
At the General Assembly in Fort Rae, James Wah-Shee, president of the Indian Brotherhood, submits his resignation. (Richard Nerysoo is acting-president until July, 1976.)

"This Land is Not For Sale", by Hugh and Karmel McCullum and John Olthuis is published by Anglican Book Centre, Toronto.

1976

January
An alcohol rehabilitation centre and a bush camp, Dehchinta, open in Fort Simpson.

The Territorial Council proposes changes to general hunting licence requirements. Dene chiefs object on the grounds that the changes would violate treaty rights.

The Science Council of Canada states that a Mackenzie Valley pipeline is the worst thing that could happen to the Canadian North and its people.

Elizabeth Mackenzie of Fort Rae becomes the first Dene woman Justice of the Peace, followed by Harriet Geddes of Fort Providence, appointed in August.

March
"Native Land Claims Week". Dene and Inuit speak across Canada.

George Barnaby resigns from Territorial Council.

Eleven spokesmen for the Dene tour Canadian universities and speak about land claims.

April
Judd Buchanan rejects the Dene Declaration.

Nahanni National Park Reserve is announced.

For the first time in Dene history, the Métis and Treaty Dene together elect a chief, Charlie Barnaby, in Fort Good Hope.

The Cabinet authorizes Dome Petroleum to begin open water drilling in the Beaufort Sea.

May
James Wah-Shee resigns from Territorial Council.

Five major Canadian churches sponsor a "listening conference." Church people hear of the needs and aspirations of the Native people.

June
The Native Communications Society holds its first annual General Assembly in Fort Providence and elects its first board of directors.

The film "I Was Born Here", produced by René Fumoleau is released (with a French version in 1977.)

July
At the Fort Norman General Assembly, Georges Erasmus is elected president of the Indian Brotherhood and George Barnaby, vice-president.

The executive of the Métis Association rejects the Dene proposal to form only one association, and on the last day of the Berger Hearings, favours building the Mackenzie Valley Pipeline as soon as possible.

Rae-Edzo votes for liquor prohibition.

A government policy paper "New Federal Government-Indian Relationship" recognizes, "a concept of Indian identity within Canadian society rather than separation from Canadian society or assimilation into it."

August
The Berger Inquiry holds, in Dettah, the last of the community hearings.

September
Warren Allmand is named minister of Indian Affairs to replace Judd Buchanan.

The Métis Association rejects Dene claims based on the Dene Declaration and receives federal funding to develop a separate claim.

October
The General Assembly of the Indian Brotherhood in Fort Simpson passes a resolution to admit non-status Dene into membership. It finalizes the "Agree-

ment-In-Principle" and on October 25, the Dene present it to the federal government.

The RCMP tries to "infiltrate and disrupt" the Indian Brotherhood. Security officer McMartin explains: "The federal government would like to see some changes in the Brotherhood."

Wally Firth, MP for the Northwest Territories, speaks against the federal government policy of sterilization for some Native women.

The Métis Association publishes "Our Métis Heritage — A Portrayal", edited by Joanne Barnaby (Overvold).

November
The Berger Inquiry hearings end November 19 after two years and 1,000 testimonies. The formal hearings yielded 32,353 pages of testimony and the community hearings 8,438 pages.

In Edmonton, 1,000 people participate in a "Citizen's Counter-Conference", challenging the views of the government and industry-sponsored Northern Development Conference, which ignores the rights of Native people.

November/December
Two southern support staff for the Indian Brotherhood report thirteen break-ins at their Ottawa home. The police attribute them to "political harassment" and refuse to assist.

December
The Department of Education of the Northwest Territories publishes "The Book of the Dene", a collection of myths and legends told by Dene elders to Father Emile Petitot in the 1800s.

The Office of Native Employment opens in Yellowknife to encourage greater participation by Native people in the government of the Northwest Territories. Jake Heron is the first staff person.

1977

January
The Supreme Court of Canada denies the Dene the right to file a "caveat" over Dene land, but does not challenge the existence of their aboriginal rights, as defined by Justice W. Morrow in September, 1973.

February
The General Assembly in Fort McPherson reaffirms the Dene's desire to see land claims settled before any more large scale exploitation of the resources takes place in the Mackenzie Valley.

James Wah-Shee joins the staff of the Métis Association as Land Claims Coordinator.

March
The village of Lac La Martre votes in favour of alcohol prohibition.

Dene delegates address the United States Senate sub-committee on Insular Affairs.

Throughout 1977, public forums, rallies, conferences and workshops in support of the Dene are organized by southern Canadians in every province.

The Indian Brotherhood and the Native Communications Society offices are broken into.

April
Baker Lake workshops on local government are cancelled. Six government employees resign to protest what they feel is a deliberate attempt to teach the Natives only what the government wants them to know.

Internal strategy papers taken from the Indian Brotherhood office during the break-in are published in the Edmonton Journal and St. John's Report.

May
The minister of Indian Affairs Warren Allmand is very receptive to the Dene Nation position on land claims.

Justice Thomas Berger's report is released. He recommends postponement of the Mackenzie Valley pipeline for ten years.

The Environmental Committee of the US Government favours delaying the Mackenzie Valley pipeline.

The Dene Nation and Inuit Tapirisat of Canada affirm their mutual support and approve of the Berger Inquiry recommendations.

The Métis Association plans a meeting to discuss union with the Dene, but the pipeline issue presents an obstacle to union and the Dene chiefs do not attend.

June
The Dene National Assembly at Fort Fitzgerald officially opens membership in the Dene Nation to Métis and non-status Dene.

July
The National Energy Board rejects the Mackenzie Valley pipeline route and recommends the building of an Alaska Highway natural gas pipeline through the Yukon. This route is approved by the Canadian government in August, by President Carter in November, and by the US House of Representatives in December.

The Dogrib Dene in Rae, Lac La Martre and Rae Lakes refuse "treaty annuity" unless the government recognizes that the Dene did not "cede and surrender" their land by Treaty 11.

Following Rick Hardy's resignation, Charles Overvold is elected president of the NWT Métis Association. Joe Mercredi is elected vice-president.

Founding conference of the Native Women's Association of the Northwest Territories. Bertha Allen is elected president and continues in this position up to the present.

August
Bertha Allen is elected president of the Native Women's Association of Canada.

The Department of Indian and Northern Affairs grants Shell Canada permission to do seismic work in the Little Buffalo River area, near Fort Resolution, without the consent or consultation with the people of the area. The Fort Resolution settlement council, band council, hunters and trappers association and Métis local oppose this decision.

Charles M. (Bud) Drury is appointed by Prime Minister Trudeau as his special representative for constitutional development in the NWT. The Dene decide not to participate in the Drury Inquiry.

The Territorial Council publishes a series of booklets on the Brotherhood. Some titles are:

"Excuse us for being blunt, but we really feel that the Indian Brotherhood of the Northwest Territories should be renamed the Radical Left.

"We appreciate that Canadian churches mean well by supporting the Indian Brotherhood of the Northwest Territories. Frankly, though, we believe the churches have been conned.

"You've heard from the radical few about Canada's North . . . Now hear from the moderate many".

The Spring and Summer of 1977 see an avalanche of similar writings in local newspapers and in the St. John's Calgary Report.

September
Ottawa southern support office closes and Project North assumes all responsibility for southern support.

Georges Erasmus and Francois Paulette of the Dene Nation address the International Non-Governmental Organizations (INGO) Conference sponsored by the United Nations in Geneva, Switzerland. Marie Helene Laraque (Paulette) who helped organize the conference also attends with son Noni, 6 weeks old, the youngest participant.

Fort Franklin votes to prohibit liquor in the community.

The NWT Métis Association presents, "Our Land, Our Culture, Our Future" to the federal government as their proposed "claims agreement".

Indian Affairs Minister Warren Allmand is replaced by Hugh Faulkner.

October
In Fort Smith, the Dene begin a Cultural Revival course.

November
The Indian Brotherhood and its resource group of five "white advisors" jointly announce that the resource group ceases as Indian Brotherhood employees because of a "disagreement over the work priority now before the organization".

The minister of Indian Affairs appoints Keith Penner as his personal representative for land claims negotiations, across Canada.

December
The Métis of the Northwest Territories

assure Penner of their willingness to participate in joint negotiations with the Dene and federal government.

Fort Resolution people refuse services to government employees for two days to protest the territorial government's refusal to fund their local sawmill. Finally, plans are made to turn control of the sawmill to the people of Fort Resolution.

The Métis Development Corporation establishes its head office in Norman Wells. The office will move to Fort Smith in 1981 and Jake Heron will become the general manager.

The World Council of Churches' Fund to Combat Racism grants $15,000 to the Dene Nation. Similar grants will be given yearly.

The book "Moratorium: Justice, Energy, the North and Native People", by Hugh and Karmel McCullum and John Olthuis is published by Anglican Book Centre, Toronto.

Phil G. Howard, of the Northern Canada Evangelical Mission, completes a dictionary of Slavey verbs. In the 1950s he had developed a Roman orthography for writing the Slavey language.

Victor P. Monus, of the Wycliffe Bible Translators, completes a dictionary of Slavey nouns. Since 1973 he has been translating the New Testament into Slavey.

1978

January
Keith Penner, of the Office of Native Claims, tells the Dene chiefs in Fort Providence that he would negotiate with the Mackenzie Valley chiefs if there was no progress with the Indian Brotherhood, because "the minister has no obligation to meet with the Native associations, the obligation is to the Indian chiefs".

The Native Women's Association trains seven workers to promote the recruitment of Native foster parents in the communities.

Fort Franklin people and Chief George Kodakin issue a declaration of independence from the Northwest Territories government. "We want to work our way according to our laws."

Faulkner offers the Dene a James Bay-like settlement, including up to $250 million in cash, and reserve-like land from 75,000 to 125,000 square kilometres for their traditional or economic use, but with no rights or control over non-renewable resources or water, and no surface or sub-surface rights. The Dene describe that offer as "totally ludicrous". The Métis say the offer is based on a "beads and trinkets philosophy". Negotiations with the federal government stop until 1981.

February
The Métis Association hires Harold Cook to replace Jim Evans as land claims negotiator.

The Canadian Arctic Resources Committee (CARC) holds a conference in Edmonton, with strong Dene participation.

March
Dene National Assembly in Fort Franklin. The "Dene Nation" is formally proclaimed.

April
After three years of operation, the "Joint Cabinet — National Indian Brotherhood Committee" is dissolved as the government saw it as an "advisory" body and the Brotherhood considered it to be a "negotiating" power.

May
Herb Norwegian and Bob Overvold tour major West German cities on a six week education tour.

The Dene successfully oppose the Canadian Coast Guard plan to spray in the Mackenzie Valley, the same defoliants which were used by the United States Army to destroy vegetation in Vietnam.

June
Four hundred and fifty Dene meet in Lac La Martre to discuss unity with the Métis.

The Dene at Rae, Rae Lakes, Lac La Martre, Fort Good Hope, Colville Lake, and Fort Franklin refuse the annual treaty annuity offered by the Department of Indian Affairs.

Seventy-six Native people have graduated in the Native Teacher Education Program established in 1968.

At the age of ninety-three, Julian Yendo of Wrigley dies. He was the last survivor of the Dene chiefs who reportedly signed Treaty 11 in 1921.

The community of Snowdrift votes in favour of alcohol prohibition.

August
Dene National Assembly in Fort Norman. Over one thousand Dene meet to discuss unity with the Métis. Georges Erasmus is re-elected president of the Dene Nation, with vice presidents George Blondin and Richard Nerysoo.

September
Faulkner cuts off all loans for negotiations to the Métis Association and the Dene Nation.

After two years of rationing, Fort Resolution votes in favour of alcohol prohibition, the sixth Dene community and the eleventh in the Northwest Territories to do so.

October
Fort Good Hope votes in favour of alcohol prohibition.

Sam Raddi, president of COPE, and Hugh Faulkner, minister of Indian and Northern Affairs, sign an Agreement-in-Principle establishing the basis for settlement of the COPE Claim over 435,000 square kilometres.

November
The Alberta Government announces plans to proceed with feasibility studies on the construction of the hydro-electric dam on the Slave River, near the Alberta-Northwest Territories border even though the people of the area oppose the project.

In Victoria, Regina and Saskatoon, the Dene take part in activities to raise support for the Dene Nation.

1979

January
The Nats'enelu Society is formed in Fort Simpson to promote the creation and exhibition of high quality traditional handicrafts.

March
Georges Erasmus is nominated NDP candidate in the Western Arctic for the upcoming federal election. He loses the seat by a narrow margin.

Project North organizes the "Northern Native Rights Campaign" across Canada. Participants include the Dene Nation, Council for Yukon Indians, and Inuit Tapirisat of Canada.

The Dene Nation voices support for Nunavut, the Inuit Tapirisat of Canada proposal for self-government in the Eastern Arctic.

Bob Overvold, Aboriginal Rights Director for the Dene Nation, addresses the Territorial Council and praises "the new and positive relationship" between the Dene Nation and the new council.

Successful winter for over 1,800 trappers in Denendeh.

In Fort Rae, a new radio station transmits a daily one-hour program in the Dogrib language under the direction of the local Native Women's Association.

April
Stuart Hodgson, Commissioner of the Northwest Territories, resigns.

Raymond Yakeleya, a Slavey from Fort Norman, produces "We Remember", the first film directed by a Dene. The film wins the "Best Documentary" award at the American Indian Film Festival in San Francisco in 1980.

Innu, Dene, Nishga, and Yukon Indians organize an information campaign in southern Canada.

The film "Dene Nation", produced by the Dene and directed by René Fumoleau, is released.

The Prince of Wales Northern Heritage Centre opens in Yellowknife.

Métis and Dene leaders meet in Inuvik and agree to form one negotiating team comprised of the Métis local presidents and the Dene chiefs.

Four hundred and fifty Canadian Indians take part in an Indian Government conference in Montreal.

June
The Hunters and Trappers Associations form a territorial wide association with

Leo Norwegian as president.

Jake Epp is appointed minister of Indian and Northern Affairs in the Progressive Conservative government led by Prime Minister Joe Clark.

Three hundred and forty Indian leaders, chiefs and elders, including Dene President Georges Erasmus, travel to London, England, to request Prime Minister Thatcher and the Queen to support their demand to participate in the Canadian constitutional debate. At the request of Prime Minister Joe Clark, London does not grant them an interview.

July

In Fort Resolution, Dene and Métis delegates from nearly all communities, propose to work towards unity. Later in the month, the Métis Assembly in Fort Smith rejects the proposal in favour of maintaining separate organizations with close ties.

Fort Good Hope, Colville Lake and Fort Franklin boycott the annual treaty ceremony.

August

The Dene National Assembly takes place in Fort Providence. Herb Norwegian is elected vice-president, the first Non-status Dene to hold executive office.

James Ross publishes "Dinjii Zhuh Dene Games", a booklet introducing seven traditional Loucheux games.

The Dempster Highway is officially opened.

September

In Fort Smith, children from kindergarten to grade three are offered the Cree and Chipewyan languages as part of the curriculum.

October

A majority of Natives (Dene, Métis and Inuit) are elected to the Territorial Council. James Wah-Shee and Richard Nerysoo head government departments.

The National Indian Brotherhood executive council (including Georges Erasmus), meets with Prime Minister Joe Clark, and demands participation in the constitutional talks.

November

The Dene Nation organizes a community development training program involving historical research, education, development and communication. Nine trainees follow this program in Fort Good Hope, with Joanne Barnaby (Overvold) as co-ordinator.

Judge Patrick Mahoney rules that the Baker Lake area is subject to Inuit aboriginal rights, thereby establishing aboriginal rights in the Canadian legal system for the first time.

Fort Good Hope replaces its band council and settlement council with a unified Dene Council. Aklavik takes similar action in April 1980. More communities follow.

1980

January

Sixty-five Dene chiefs and delegates meet in Fort Franklin. They call on the federal government to reopen negotiations, at a standstill for the past two years.

February/March

Esso Resources Canada plans to expand oilfield production at Norman Wells, disregarding the Berger Inquiry recommendations. Interprovincial Pipe Lines plans to construct an 866 km. pipeline throughout Denendeh from Norman Wells to Zama, Alberta.

March

John Munro is appointed Minister of Indian and Northern Affairs, when the Liberals form a new government.

Jim Bourque is elected president of the Métis Association.

Bud Drury releases his report on constitutional development in the Northwest Territories.

April

"First Nations Constitutional Conference" in Ottawa.

May

Thirty Dene travel to Ottawa to lobby against the Norman Wells project.

June

The Legislative Assembly of the Northwest Territories passes a motion to oppose the Norman Wells project until land claims negotiations have reached an acceptable stage.

The first Northwest Territories conference on alcohol abuse is held in Snowdrift.

The Legislative Assembly of the Northwest Territories recommends recognition of aboriginal rights, and supports the Native groups in the negotiating process.

The "Dene Nation Newsletter" begins publication out of the Dene national office.

July

Cece McCauley, formerly of Fort Norman, is elected Dene chief in Inuvik, the first woman chief in Denendeh.

The minister of Indian Affairs allows individual bands in Canada to decide whether or not Indian women may retain their status when marrying a non-Indian.

Treaty Dene and Métis take part in the Dene National Assembly in Fort Good Hope. Georges Erasmus is re-elected president for a third term. Herb Norwegian and Paul Andrew are elected vice-presidents. The Métis Declaration of Rights is passed at this assembly. The Dene decide to participate in the Territorial Government, even though it is not "the most appropriate form of government for Native people." The name Denendeh was discussed as the name for the Dene homeland.

August

The National Indian Brotherhood supports the Dene in their opposition to the "imposed development" of the Norman Wells project. They also reject "observer status" offered to the Indians for the debate on the Canadian Constitution.

Snowdrift, Fort Good Hope and Fort Smith boycott treaty annuities.

September

The Third annual Native Women's conference is held in Yellowknife. The theme is "Preserving Dene Culture".

The Nishi Khon Centre opens in Rae, containing government offices, laundromat, post office, radio station, courthouse, beauty parlour, store, and coffee shop.

October

Thirty Dene travel to Edmonton to speak at the National Energy Board hearings on the Norman Wells pipeline. All but one are refused permission to speak. Herb Norwegian, vice-president of the Dene Nation, again asks for a delay of the project.

November

The international "Russell Tribunal on the Rights of the Indians of the North and Latin America" during its session in Rotterdam, Holland, finds Canada guilty of the theft of Indian lands, water, and natural resources, and guilty of trying to destroy a way of life.

The Dene ask the minister of Indian Affairs to turn forest fire fighting responsibilities over to them.

The Legislative Assembly recommends division of the Northwest Territories into two political jurisdictions, subject to a plebiscite.

December

At the second "First Nations Constitutional Conference", over one thousand Indians from every province and territory, including 350 chiefs, tell Prime Minister Trudeau: "We are nations, and we are going into the world community to be recognized by nations."

Bill C-48, the new Canadian energy bill, is given first reading in the House of Commons.

The Native Women's Association opens a center in Yellowknife to promote the ethnic pride and cultural heritage of the Native people and to market their arts and crafts.

1981

January

The Environmental Assessment Panel recommends beginning construction on the Norman Wells pipeline project in 1982 if certain economic and environmental deficiencies are corrected.

February

Fort Simpson implements liquor rationing.

Representatives from the Northwest Territories, Manitoba, and Saskatchewan form a Caribou Management Board.

Georges Erasmus and Dave Porter of CYI address the Legislative Assembly and state "if Bill C-48 is passed, it will be the biggest land grab in history".

COPE negotiations halt. The government wishes to change some of the Agreement-in-Principle signed between COPE and Canada on October 31, 1978.

The Native Council of Canada supports the governments of the Northwest Territories and Yukon, and the Métis and Dene in their united opposition to Bill C-48.

The special joint committee on the Constitution recognizes and affirms existing aboriginal rights for all Indians, Inuit, and Métis in Canada.

March
A health conference, initiated by the Dene Nation and the Native Women's Association, is held in Rae-Edzo.

The Dene Nation and the council for Yukon Indians are granted a broadcasting licence by the CRTC.

The Fort Liard Dene Band asks the Department of Indian Affairs for a 142,000 square kilometre reserve.

April
The federal government appoints David Osborn as federal negotiator for the Dene Métis claim.

A report, "Native People and the Constitution of Canada" is released by the Métis and Non-Status Constitutional Review Commission.

Filming begins on "The Last Mooseskin Boat", directed by Raymond Yakeleya, and produced by the Native Communications Society and the National Film Board.

May
Jim Bourque, President of the Métis Association, and other delegates of the Native Council of Canada attend a World Council of Indigenous Peoples' Conference in Australia.

The National Energy Board approves the Norman Wells Pipeline project.

The Dene Nation, Métis Association, Committee for Justice and Liberty, and Canadian Arctic Resources Committee make application to take the National Energy Board to court over the Norman Wells pipeline decision. The application is denied.

The Adult Vocational Training Centre (AVTC) in Fort Smith becomes Thebacha College.

June
Dene/Métis leadership meeting at Rae Lakes. Federal negotiator, David Osborn, attends.

July
The aboriginal rights negotiations begin with David Osborn, but close the same day because of the government decision to approve the Norman Wells project.

Northwest Territories delegates attend the Native Council of Canada meeting in Ottawa to voice concerns over the pending patriation of the Constitution.

The Cabinet approves the Norman Wells project. Munro promises the Dene a two year delay in construction, and $18 million to prepare for the impact.

Almost half of the Dene bands boycott the annual treaty ceremonies.

August
Slavey language is used in Fort Providence, Fort Franklin and Fort Good Hope schools. Fort Norman, Fort Resolution, Lac La Martre, Dettah, Hay River, and Fort Smith will use Dene textbooks in 1982.

Negotiations with the federal negotiator resume.

September
Herb Norwegian, Jim Antoine, and Frank T'Seleie attend an international conference on the rights of indigenous people in Geneva, Switzerland.

October
The territorial government presents, "Our Land, Our Future", a proposal for the political evolution of the Northwest Territories.

November
The Dene Nation releases its document, "Public Government for the People of the North", known as the "Denendeh Proposal".

Esso Resources begins construction of four artificial islands in the Mackenzie River at Norman Wells.

The Prime Minister, due to pressure from provincial Premiers, removes clause 34, recognizing aboriginal rights from The Constitutional Charter of Rights.

The Dene oppose government of Alberta plans to divert the waters of the Peace, Athabasca, and Slave Rivers to flow south rather than into the Northwest Territories.

Georges Erasmus leads a coalition of Native groups in Ottawa fighting for the recognition of aboriginal rights in the Canadian Constitution. The Legislative Assembly reconvenes in Ottawa and provides remarkable support.

December
The House of Commons recognizes the existing aboriginal and treaty rights, in the Canadian Constitution.

Bill C-48 receives final assent in the House of Commons.

1982

January
The first conference on constitutional development in the western Northwest Territories is organized by the Legislative Assembly.

Citizens for Public Justice (CPJ) distributes across Canada 100,000 pamphlets explaining the Denendeh Proposal.

The Métis Association, Dene Nation, and Native Communications Society launch a one-hour pilot radio program "Datsedi" in Dene and English languages.

The Dene Arts Resource Centre is opened by the Native Women's Association, in Yellowknife.

February
A Constitutional Alliance is formed with representatives from the eastern and western Northwest Territories and all northern Native organizations.

The Native Communications Society trains Dene to broadcast in radio, and television.

Jim Bourque resigns as Métis Association president. He achieved more co-operation than ever before between the Métis Association and Dene Nation. He becomes deputy minister of the Department of Renewable Resources.

The first Slavey language interpreter is hired by the Legislative Assembly.

March
The Native Women's Association begins the pre-employment training courses.

March/April
Dene National Assembly in Fort Simpson.

April
Thirteen Dene attend a national Indian conference in Penticton, B.C. The Assembly of First Nations is organized to replace the National Indian Brotherhood.

A plebiscite indicates that the majority of people of the Northwest Territories want the territories divided into two political jurisdictions, one in the east, one in the west.

June
The Western and Nunavut Constitutional forums are established.

July
The World Assembly of First Nations is held in Regina, Saskatchewan.

August
Dene National Assembly in Fort McPherson.

General Assembly of the Métis Association in Inuvik. Bob Stevenson is elected president.

October
"Focus North", the first northern produced CBC public affairs television program goes on the air, with host Marie Wilson. It is telecast in English, Inuktitut, and Slavey languages.

November
Following a four month breakdown, negotiations reopen between the Dene, Métis, and federal government.

The Slave River Basin coalition is formed with the theme, "Survival on the Slave" (SOS), and opposition to the building of the Slave River dam.

1983

March

A First Ministers' Conference on Aboriginal Rights in the Constitution is held in Ottawa.

April

Dene Nation, Métis Association, and Esso Resources form Sheetah Drilling to participate in the Norman Wells expansion project.

July

Wally Firth is elected President of the Metis Association.

August

The Assembly of the World Council of Churches in Vancouver strongly support aboriginal rights.

Archbishop Edward Scott, Primate of the Anglican Church asks the Federal Government to give Native people full title to their land.

The Métis and Dene agree on eligibility for aboriginal claims.

The Legislative Assembly and the Dene Nation oppose testing of the cruise missiles in the Mackenzie Valley.

Dene National Assembly in Fort Resolution. Stephen Kakfwi is elected president with Roy Fabian and Charlie Snowshoe, vice-presidents.

October

Bob Overvold is selected as chief negotiator for the Dene and Metis.

Georges Erasmus is appointed vice-chief of the Assembly of First Nations.

The Parliamentary Special Committee on Indian Affairs publishes its report "Indian Self Government in Canada".

November

Voters in the Northwest Territories elect fourteen Natives to the 24-seat Legislative Assembly.

December

The Beaufort Sea Environment Assessment Review Board holds public meetings in the Mackenzie Valley.

1984

January

Nick Sibbeston is chosen to be Minister of Local Government and Culture, and Associate Minister of Aboriginal Rights and Constitutional Development.

Richard Nerysoo is the first Native person to be chosen as Government Leader by the Executive Council of the Government of the Northwest Territories.

The Western Constitutional Forum and a group of Dene hold a conference in Rae-Edzo on the traditional Dene model of government and its implications for the political development of the Northwest Territories.

James Wah-Shee is chosen as Deputy Speaker of the Legislative Assembly of the Northwest Territories.

Work begins on the pipeline from Norman Wells to Zama. Construction period will be three months this winter, and three months in winter 1984-1985.

Attorneys-general, justice ministers and national Native leaders meet in Yellowknife to plan the First Ministers' Conference on Aboriginal Rights to be held in March. Native leaders condemn the federal government policy of extinguishment of aboriginal rights.

The Government of the Northwest Territories recognizes the "Fort Good Hope Assembly" as an official one-council government system.

Wally Firth resigns as president of the Metis Association for health reasons. The board executive appoints Larry Tourangeau as president.

February

The Government of the Northwest Territories publishes a report "On Cultural Needs".

The newly formed Dogrib Tribal Council plans to form a regional development corporation.

Members of the Nunavut and Western Constitutional Forums set the process and the criteria for the choice of a boundary to divide the Northwest Territories.

The federal government announces a $130 million program to prepare for the production and transportation of Beaufort Sea oil and gas.

Anti-trapping campaigns are organized in Canada and Europe.

James Wah-Shee is elected president of the Western Arctic Liberal Association.

Nick Sibbeston is named chairman of the Western Constitutional Forum.

March

Second National Constitutional Conference on Aboriginal Rights in Ottawa.

Despite the continued opposition of the Dene and of many other Canadians, the first cruise missile test takes place along the Mackenzie Valley.

The Alaska Native Review Commission begins hearings in Anchorage on the 1971 Alaska Native Claims Settlement Act. It is chaired by Thomas Berger.

The Committee for Original People's Entitlement (COPE) and the Council for Yukon Indians (CYI) come to an agreement on the overlap lands of their claims.

COPE and the Dene and Métis reach an agreement on the overlap areas of their claims.

The Federal Cabinet approves the COPE land claims proposal.

Following the desire of Pope John Paul II to meet Canadian Native people, the four major Canadian Native organizations agree to invite him to Fort Simpson, in Denendeh, on September 18, 1984.

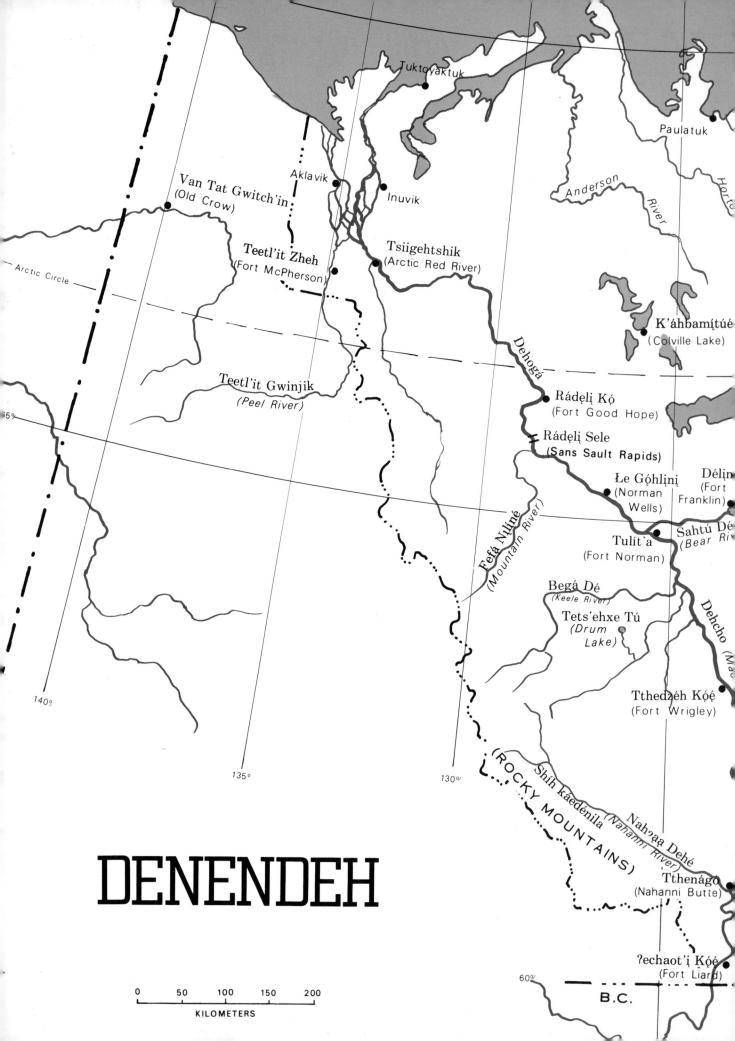

Tuktoyaktuk

Paulatuk

Anderson River

Harto

Van Tat Gwitch'in
(Old Crow)

Aklavik

Inuvik

Teetl'it Zheh
(Fort McPherson)

Tsiigehtshik
(Arctic Red River)

Arctic Circle

Dehogá

K'áhbamítúé
(Colville Lake)

Teetl'it Gwinjik
(Peel River)

Rádeli Kó
(Fort Good Hope)

65°

Rádeli Sele
(Sans Sault Rapids)

Łe Góhlini
(Norman Wells)

Délı̨
(Fort
Franklin)

Fefá Nı̨lı̨né
(Mountain River)

Sahtú Dé
(Bear Ri

Tulít'a
(Fort Norman)

Begá Dé
(Keele River)

Dehcho (Ma

Tets'ehxe Tú
(Drum Lake)

Tthedzéh Kóé
(Fort Wrigley)

140°

135°

130°

Shíh k̓aedénila (Nahanni River)

(ROCKY MOUNTAINS)

Nahʔaa Dehé

Tthenágo
(Nahanni Butte)

DENENDEH

ʔechaot'i Kóé
(Fort Liard)

60°

B.C.

0   50   100   150   200
KILOMETERS